THE·JOY·OF·AROMATHERAPY

THE·JOY·OF Aromatherapy

Sensual remedies for everyday ailments

CATHY HOPKINS

An Imprint of HarperCollins*Publishers*

AN ANGUS & ROBERTSON BOOK

First published in the United Kingdom by
Angus & Robertson (UK) in 1991
An imprint of HarperCollinsPublishers Ltd
First published in Australia by
Collins/Angus & Robertson Australia in 1991
A division of HarperCollinsPublishers
(Australia) Pty Ltd

Angus & Robertson (UK)
77–85 Fulham Palace Road, London W6 8JB
United Kingdom
Collins/Angus & Robertson Publishers Australia
Unit 4, Eden Park, 31 Waterloo Road,
North Ryde, NSW 2113, Australia
William Collins Publishers Ltd
31 View Road, Glenfield, Auckland 10,
New Zealand

British Library Cataloguing in Publication Data
Hopkins, Cathy
The joy of aromatherapy.
1. Health. Use of Aromatic compounds
I. Title
615.32

ISBN 0–207–16871–7

Printed in Finland
Typeset in the UK by The Wordshop,
Bury, Lancs

With special thanks . . .

. . . to Nicole Perez for sharing her passion and knowledge of the oils with her students in such a colourful and informative way on her training courses. To my mother for wading through my handwritten scripts and making sense of them and my father for patiently typing them out. Also to my editor Valerie Hudson and my husband Steve for their consistent encouragement and support.

CONTENTS

INTRODUCTION

The joy of aromatherapy is that anyone, anywhere can benefit. As for every nettle sting there is a dock leaf growing nearby to soothe it, so in creation there is a remedy for every ailment – one that is potent and yet completely pure.

Aromatherapy is an age-old treatment known to many of the earliest civilizations. The essential oils which it uses are extracted from flowers, leaves, fruit, tree bark, roots and wood. What could be more natural? Each oil has its own individual scent and healing potential. Eucalyptus is well known to most of us for its ability to alleviate a cold or a sore chest, but there are many more oils for just about every complaint you could imagine – headaches, wrinkles, PMT, cellulite, gout, insomnia . . . the list goes on and on. You do not need to be a trained aromatherapist to benefit from the use of essential oils in your own home, although if you are in doubt about any aspect of aromatherapy you should consult one, particularly if you have a serious condition. Otherwise, at your fingertips is nature's gift – simple, easily available and a pure joy.

It is a number of years since aromatherapy first aroused public interest as a treatment for both health and beauty. Several excellent books on the subject have already been published. So why another now?

Many previous writers were particularly concerned to see

aromatherapy recognized for the wonderful and potent treatment it is, and so enable it to take its place as an authentic holistic therapy. As a result they presented their case in as academic and scientific manner as they could. They emphasized the research that had been undertaken, and went into great detail about the subject's vast and fascinating history. Whilst this makes interesting reading for some, especially for serious students and practitioners, many people have complained to me that they got lost in the complexities of these text books and gave up. All they wanted to know was; What can I do if I've got a headache? Are there any dangers? How do I mix the oils? But after wading their way through chapters with titles such as 'The chemical components of the oils and methods of extraction' they abandoned their search.

My intention in writing this book, therefore, is to make aromatherapy as accessible as possible to someone who knows nothing about the subject and yet would like to learn about the oils and how to use them. My aim has been to produce an easy-to-follow manual and to point people in the right direction for safe home use.

In the first chapter I have tried to answer all the questions people always ask about the oils and the treatment. Chapters 2–7 then deal with different areas within our lives where aromatherapy can be used, and give simple recipes. Chapter 2 outlines a starter kit. As there are almost three hundred essential oils, all with different properties, the newcomer to aromatherapy is often stumped about where to begin. I have chosen twelve oils which I believe will be of maximum benefit to someone using them at home, and I have described ways in which they can be used and combined with other oils.

Chapter 3 emphasizes the importance of recognizing stress and the different ways it manifests itself, and shows how to use aromatherapy to prevent it developing into a major problem. Chapter 4 offers some practical tips for skin and hair care and lists ways to revive and rejuvenate a weary skin. Chapter 5 is specifically for and about women. There are so many ways the oils can assist with various women's problems, from PMT through to pregnancy, post-natal depression and the menopause. This chapter offers some handy tips for various conditions or disorders and gives recipes for regular use.

Chapter 6 describes how the oils, many of which are diuretic and detoxifying, can assist a cleansing or slimming programme. Chapter 7 covers the sensual side of aromatherapy. Many of the oils are known to be aphrodisiacs; at the very least, they can help you relax and feel mellow. This chapter gives hints for creating an atmosphere conducive to sensuality and describes ways in which the aromas can evoke and enhance arousal and so improve your sex life.

Chapters 8 and 9 are intended for quick and easy reference. An A–Z of oils and their properties is followed by an A–Z of minor disorders, appropriate oils and methods of application. A list of suppliers and courses, and a recommended reading list, complete this practical section.

So now, enjoy your discovery of the oils. I am sure you won't look back.

SOME BASIC QUESTIONS ANSWERED

What exactly is aromatherapy?

A wonderful, nourishing and luxurious experience, aromatherapy is a therapeutic treatment using essential oils and massage. It is the only treatment that actually combines remedies with hands-on therapy and body work.

Through their unique character, smell and healing properties, the oils have a psychological as well as a physical effect. They can be used for both health and beauty as they restore balance and encourage the body's own healing power, so enhancing the user's look and feeling of well-being.

Although aromatherapy can help many ailments, its original and most effective use is as a preventative rather than a curative treatment. As Hippocrates said: 'The way to health is to have an aromatic bath and scented massage every day.' As a regular treatment, aromatherapy can keep the body relaxed, balanced and in harmony – which is the first step to good health. Rather than turning to it when you are drained, worn-out and tense and wanting a treatment to 'fix' the hurt, it is better to incorporate the use of oils into your daily and weekly routine so that you will never get into that state in the first place.

What are the origins of aromatherapy?

To many of us in the late twentieth century aromatherapy appears to be a new form of treatment which has emerged only in the last decade or so. Yet the use of essential oils was known thousands of years ago in the ancient civilizations of Egypt, China, Greece, Rome, India and Arabia. What happened then and since is a fascinating story worthy of a whole book in itself. There are references to the aromatic oils in art and literature from many different cultures throughout the ages, and yet to so many people these days aromatherapy is still considered 'just another new fad'.

References to their use in Egypt for cosmetics, medicinal purposes and embalming can be found from as far back as 4500 BC. Traces of cedarwood, clove, nutmeg and cinnamon have been found impregnated in mummies' bandages (although it should be said that only the Pharaohs and upper classes were mummified, the others being dumped in a communal pit!). In 1922, vases fragrant with aromatic oils were found in the tomb of the boy-king Tutankhamun (1361–1352 BC). Cleopatra was said to have seduced Antony with her knowledge of the aphrodisiac potency of some of the oils. She bathed in jasmine, had her floors strewn with carpets of rose petals and her barges garlanded with flowers. Shakespeare wrote of them 'purple the sails and so perfumed that the winds were lovesick with them'. In fact it was common practice amongst Egyptian women to use aromatic oils firstly in the bath, then for massage by slaves. In those days, Egyptian perfume had the same reputation that the French product has today, although in those ancient times the scents would be made from natural essences and, as well as smelling good, were also protective to the body. Nowadays, most perfumes are synthesized in the laboratory.

Hieroglyphics show the ancient Egyptians burning oils at different times, sometimes to the gods (frankincense to the sun, myrrh to the moon) and sometimes at different times of day to suit different needs, for instance to create an energetic mood in time of war or a tranquil outlook in situations requiring serenity. We now know that some of the oils can invigorate or stimulate (ideal in the early part of the day to prepare us 'for going into battle', as it were) whilst others have the power to relax and calm us (perfect for evenings and for times when we simply wish to be quiet and still). The Egyptians also blended oils for relieving a variety of illnesses.

The traditional ayurvedic medicine of India is three thousand years old and aromatic massage is one of its principal aspects. Aromatic herbs and woods are used to make up infused oils with which to massage the body. In ancient China, natural medicine was also the norm and *The Yellow Emperor's Classic of Internal Medicine*, written about 2650 BC, contains references to the oils.

The use of aromatic oils gradually spread to ancient Greece and Rome. It appears that in those days the oils were precious and highly valued, presented as gifts to the gods and esteemed guests and hosts in much the same way that we might give wine, flowers or chocolates today. The perfumes were also used as part of great festivities. At the games held in Daphne, a king of Syria who ruled from 175–164 BC had a procession of beauties carrying golden bowls of perfume to sprinkle onto the spectators; thousands of special guests were given spikenard, lily, cinnamon, saffron and, as a parting gift, frankincense and myrrh.

In the days of the poet Ovid, round about the time of Christ, Rome had as many perfume shops as Greece. For example, in Capra there was a whole street of shops selling fashionable oils imported from Egypt. Petronius wrote: 'Wives are out of fashion; mistresses are in; rose leaves now are dated; now cinnamon's the thing'! The Roman Emperor Nero was also known for his love of scent, and concealed pipes in his palace to spray his guests with fragrant perfumes. A few hundred years later, in the fifth and sixth centuries BC, the Greeks rivalled the Egyptians for their scented extravagance. 'Each guest upon his forehead bears a wreathed flowery crown. From slender vase a willing youth presents to each in turn a costly perfume while odorous gums fill all the room.' It was also the custom to saturate birds' wings in perfume and have them fly about, so scenting the air.

The ancient Greeks and Romans also made liberal use of rose in wine, and ate dishes flavoured with rosewater (now known for its ability to aid digestion and for its healing effect on the liver). They used the oils both cosmetically and medicinally. The ancient physician Marestheus stated that aromatic flowers could have either sedative or stimulating properties. We now know this to be true: jasmine, for instance, uplifts, while lavender sedates.

Pedacius Dioscorides in Cicilia wrote a treatise on herbal medicine in the first century AD. One section is specifically on aromatics, and many of his findings have been confirmed by modern research. The general motto for wellbeing could be summed up as: 'The best recipe for health is to apply sweet scents to the brain.'

The knowledge of oils which had built up over thousands of years spread to Arabia, where in the eleventh century AD there lived a Persian physician called Avicenna who discovered distillation, the main method still used today to extract oils. His work *The Canon of Medicine* refers to the healing properties of the oils. Avicenna recommended massage to prepare for exercise, to treat after exercise, to increase or decrease body weight and finally to tone up the body. He wrote, 'Restorative friction produces repose. Its object is to disperse the effete matter formed in the muscles and not expelled by exercise. It causes the effete matter to disperse and so removes fatigue. Such friction is soft and gentle and is best done with oil or perfumed ointment.' We know today that massage can break down the uric and lactic acids which build up during exercise. The massage is further assisted by certain diuretic and detoxifying essential oils.

It is thought that crusading knights brought the oils and scents back with them to Europe in the Middle Ages. Here perfumed oil was often used to mask the smell of the 'great unwashed'. It was a fashion to have the hems of one's gown and gloves scented to distract one's nose from body smells, but often oils and herbs were strewn in the house for their disinfectant as well as aromatic properties.

At the time of the plague in Athens, Hippocrates urged people to burn aromatic oils to protect themselves. Centuries later, in England, Charles II did the same. Pomanders stuck with garlic and cloves were worn around the neck to ward off infection. The doctors who treated plague victims used to wear protective leather clothing consisting of a gown, gloves and a beaked mask, the latter filled with cloves, cinnamon and other spices. By breathing through this beak, the doctors hoped to remain immune from infection. Sponges were impregnated in the same spices and held under the noses of the sick. Modern research has since shown these oils to be anti-viral and anti-bacterial – cinnamon and clove being particularly effective for killing typhoid and cholera bacteria. Master Alexis of Piedmont, an alchemist of the time, wrote, 'To make a verie good perfume against the plague, you must take mastich, chypre, incense, mace, wormwood, myrrh, aloes wood, musk, ambergris, nutmegs, myrtle, bay, rosemary, sages, roses, elder, clove, juniper and pitch. All these stamped and mixed together, you shall set upon the coales and so perfume the chamber.' A potent mixture indeed! Certainly a very protective one.

It is interesting to note that the very few ships from the East that brought the rats and their fleas that carried the bubonic plague also brought the antidote – cloves and cinnamon. It is also worth observing that the largest group of people to escape the ravages of the plague were the perfumers. They rarely became ill as they were working with natural plant essences to make their scents, the antiseptic properties in which kept them protected.

Several books on aromatherapy were written in the sixteenth and seventeenth centuries. In fact, it could be said that modern aromatherapy started in Germany in the 1500s and 1600s and has taken four hundred years to achieve its present state. Hieronymus Braunschweig wrote a number of books on distillation; his last work, *New Volkomen Distillier-buch*, published in 1591, referred to twenty-five essential oils. Similar references are made by Conrad Gesner in *The Treasure of Enonynus*, published in 1559. J. J. Wecker, writing in 1616, said: 'Perfumes are certainly compound medicine which can affect the mind and eliminate all bad odours and infections in the air that surrounds us.' Today, we know that oils such as eucalyptus can prevent viruses from spreading. In the 1600s, Nicholas Culpepper in England recorded the uses of plants. He wrote, 'The oil drawn from the leaves and flowers is of sovereign help, to touch the temples and nostrils with two to three drops for all diseases of the brain; for the inward diseases it must be done with discretion, as the case requires, for it is very quick and piercing.'

Although all herbalists of the time knew of the oils, and they were used by householders who passed their knowledge down from generation to generation right into the eighteenth century, herbalism gradually began to be considered old-fashioned. The practice faded out and gave way in the face of new chemical research and synthetically prepared drugs which seemed to spell the end for plant essences.

Towards the end of the nineteenth century, however, fresh interest began to be shown in the medicinal properties of herbs. William Whitler's book *Materia Medica* of 1882 contains references to twenty-two oils. There was also mild interest in the flower-growing districts in France, where the workers were found to be completely free of respiratory infection at a time when tuberculosis was rife. In 1887, the first record was made of tests carried out to find if the oils were anti-bacterial. Chamberland in Paris in 1887 and Cadéac and Meunier in 1888 published similar studies which showed that the micro-organisms of glandular and yellow fever were easily killed by essential oils – the most effective being cinnamon, thyme, lavender and juniper. Since then, many experiments have demonstrated the anti-bacterial, anti-viral and anti-fungal effects of the oils, but the main trends have been away from plant essences and towards chemical and synthetic drugs. These trends have meant an emphasis on the curative rather than the preventative, thus setting the pattern for Western medicine with its tendency to treat symptoms rather than looking into underlying causes.

In the 1920s, the work of René Maurice Gattefosse showed that it was possible for essential oils to penetrate the skin and, via the blood and lymph system, to reach the inner organs. His book *Aromathérapie* examined the anti-microbial effects of the oils, and it is only since then that work with aromatic oils has been called 'aromatherapy'.

In the fifty years or so after 1887, hundreds of articles were published in the press. Speaking of aromatherapy, Gattefosse said, 'A therapy employing aromatics is a sphere of research opening enormous vistas to those who have started exploring it.' There is a famous story about his injuring his hand in a laboratory explosion and plunging it into a bowl of lavender oil; everyone was amazed to see how quickly and smoothly it healed. (Lavender is well known as the best oil for burns, cuts and wounds.)

Here and there, the seeds of interest were reawakening. For example, in 1939 Albert Couvneur published a book detailing the medicinal applications of the essential oils, whilst Dr H. Sztark – a French school inspector – introduced the idea of vaporizing oils in the classroom with the idea of preventing the spread of disease. In Italy in the 1920s, Giovanni Gatti and Renato Cayola looked into the psychotherapeutic value of oils and their action on the nervous system. The results of their tests indicated that the oils had enormous beneficial effects.

Then came one of the great pioneers of aromatherapy in this century. Dr Jean Valnet, an army surgeon working in Indo-China in the 1950s during the war against French colonial domination, was greatly influenced by the findings of Gattefosse. Valnet used the oils not only as antiseptics in the treatment of wounds but also in his psychiatric work with mentally disturbed patients. After the war he continued his research into the effects of the oils, and in 1964 he published what is now considered a classic textbook, *The Practice of Aromatherapy*. He then began teaching his findings to doctors who wanted to learn the medicinal value of oils both internally and externally. Thanks to his work, aromatherapy is now pharmacologically recognized in France and Switzerland and there are approximately 1500 general practitioners prescribing the oils for medicinal purposes.

At the same time that Valnet was examining the medicinal value of the oils, Madame Marguérite Maury was concentrating on their cosmetic usage and their effects on mood and emotion. As an alternative to oral application she advised applying the oils externally, diluted in vegetable oil and accompanied by massage. The results of her work were reported in her book *The Secret of Life and Youth*, and it has been claimed that it was she who revived the ancient art of the use of massage in combination with oils. Later she moved to England, where her methods and teaching have had great influence.

During the 1980s public interest in Britain awakened to many so-called 'alternative methods' to good health. People are now looking at natural ways of dealing with stress and all its symptoms, together with ways of ensuring healthy living through diet, lifestyle and relaxation. Once again, people are turning their attention to the actual causes of disease and away from simply concentrating on cures to make the symptoms go away. Now, if anything, the trend is towards ensuring that disease does not arrive in the first place. Aromatherapy has a large part to play in this, and today several schools of aromatherapy are in existence and there are many practitioners. Even the oils are beginning to make their appearance in more and more shops nationwide as demand increases; even in the mid-eighties it was still very difficult to find oils anywhere, except perhaps in obscure shops reputedly catering for 'cranks'.

In 1985, a small group of practitioners formed the International Federation of Aromatherapy which now issues regular newsletters about current issues, research findings and methods. It also often organizes lectures by members and other speakers in related fields of work. The address of the Federation is given on p. 128 for those who may wish to be placed on the mailing list. Not all aromatherapists, however, are members of the Federation – some have trained at schools outside its membership, and some have withdrawn for reasons of differences of opinion and belief. At present there is much discussion about forming a recognized national governing body to ensure an acceptable, common standard of practice and training.

And so the story continues. The research widens, the publicity is growing favourably and I am sure we shall hear more in the future of this fascinating and far-reaching treatment.

What are the oils and where do they come from?
They come from nature – from fruits, flowers, leaves, bark, wood, roots, spices and herbs. The orange tree, for instance, gives orange oil from its fruit, petitgrain from its

leaves and neroli from its flowers. All three oils have different fragrances and different healing potential.

The oil has been described as the soul, life force or hormone of the plant – basically the substance that gives it its own individual characteristics. Since the oils come from different parts of the plant, they vary in colour and intensity; for example, benzoin from the styrax benzoin tree trunk is thick, brown and gum-like, whereas lavender from flower tops is light and transparent. They also vary in fragrance – some are sweet and flowery, others woody, and yet others smell like strong disinfectant. Interestingly, although they are called essential oils they are not oily or greasy. In fact they are extremely volatile. Try putting a drop of pure lavender on a piece of blotting paper; it will disappear completely in time, leaving no 'oil' stain at all.

All the oils are natural antiseptics. Beyond that, some are antibiotic, anti-viral, anti-inflammatory, anti-bacterial, expectorant, diuretic, anti-spasmodic or anti-neuralgic; some stimulant (tonics); and still others sedative.

The oils have an extremely complex chemical structure, which is why it is virtually impossible to copy them synthetically. For example, eucalyptus consists of some 250 different constituents. Using energy from sunlight, the plant is able to construct hundreds of different chemical compounds from the air, water and constituents of the soil in which it is planted. Some of these ingredients are very basic, like oxygen, but many of the resulting compounds are very complex. These are grouped into eight main categories: acids, alcohols, aldehydes, cetones, esters, phenol, sequileperes and terperes. The unique combination in each plant gives it its perfume and therapeutic properties.

The oils are all collected at different times and different seasons. Pepper oil is extracted from unripe berries, coriander oil when the fruit is ripe. Jasmine flowers are picked at night and before the flower is one day old, and yet before sandalwood can be extracted the tree must be thirty years old and thirty feet high! The purity and scent can depend on several factors such as weather, harvest and time of picking. Oil extracted from plants grown in a natural environment such as a secluded valley is likely to be better quality than that obtained from plants grown in a polluted atmosphere.

How are the oils obtained from the plants?

Distillation: This is the most common method. Steam is passed over the leaves or flowers in a vacuum or under pressure, so the oils vaporize. When the steam is cooled the oils condense. Because they do not dissolve in water, they separate and can be easily collected.

Enfleurage: This method is often used for the higher-quality oils such as rose and jasmine. The flowers are spread on trays lined with fat or oil. Then they are left until the fat is saturated with perfume, which can take between six and seventy-two hours. The process is then repeated. The oil is obtained when the aromatic substances are separated from the fat with a solvent and then purified. The oil obtained by this method is usually of superior quality and more expensive.

Pressing: Simple pressure is often used for citrus fruits, whose oil is squeezed from the rinds. Most manufacturers now use machines as opposed to hand-pressing.

Solvent extraction: This is a complicated process involving the use of solvents such as alcohol or petroleum ether to dissolve the oil, plus various stages of heating, cooling and filtering. It is often used for gums and resins, but is probably more suited to use in the perfume industry as it is difficult to remove all trace of the solvents and so the oil is not always as pure as that obtained by other methods.

How do the oils actually work?

They work in two ways, the first of which is to do with the smell. Our sense of smell is actually ten thousand times more sensitive than our sense of taste. Think back to the last time you had a cold and your nose was stuffed up. Didn't your sense of taste go along with your sense of smell? This is because when we eat, we smell.

Behind the bridge of the nose is something called the olfactory bulb. From here, the olfactory nerve goes down into the mucus of the nasal cavity; tiny hairs extend from the olfactory nerve cells and are stimulated by smell. The process then reverses itself – from the cells (of which there are five million in the nose) – to the bulb – to the limbic system in the brain via the olfactory tract. This is connected to the hypothalmus, which governs other glands and the hormone system.

In plain English, what all that means is that when we smell something it has an immediate effect on our autonomic nervous system and our hormonal system. These systems govern fear, anger, heart rate, memory and reaction to stress. So our sense of smell has a powerful effect on us – and yet is often overlooked. A rose garden fragrant in full bloom or jasmine's heady scent at night can soothe and uplift the senses, just as petrol fumes, car parks or rotting garbage can make one feel nauseous, suffocated and repelled. According to some doctors, good health has an odour that is clean and fresh whilst bad health smells acidic or rotten, telling you that something is amiss. Aromatherapy recognizes the power of smell and uses it.

The oils all have different fragrances: some smell medicinal or menthol-like, others soothing, others flowery and yet others refreshing. There is no doubt that people are affected by the different scents, whether they believe in the power of smell or not. How many times does a whiff of perfume or the smell of a particular recipe evoke a place, time or person with total clarity? So the scent of the different essential oils can evoke and bring about different responses and states of mind from sedation to revival. For example, lavender can soothe, rosemary revive, rose rebalance and basil clear the head.

The second way the oils work is by entering the system and the bloodstream: through the lungs in the case of inhalation, through the skin in the case of baths, massage and compresses. As the blood circulates, the oils get transported round all the organs, which benefit from their passing through. The oil molecules are small enough to be absorbed by the skin. Some of the oils have a special affinity with a particular organ, and on reaching that organ will be deposited there. In the same way that the body uses vitamins and minerals, the organs or glands in need of help take up, selectively, the appropriate oil. Any that is left is eliminated through the normal channels – exhalation, sweat, urine and faeces.

The oils remain in the body for a number of hours and trigger off a healing process that can continue for days. This is perhaps why so many people claim that they feel brighter and revitalized the day after an aromatherapy treatment.

How can the oils help?

The benefits are many and varied. These days, good health is known to be a combination of balance between mind, body and spirit. If the state of mind is under stress it can affect the body, for example with headaches, ulcers or insomnia; if the spirit is low, it too can affect the body – just look at the posture of someone who is miserable, drained or depressed.

Aromatherapy is a treatment that relaxes both mind and body. It can result in increased vitality and improved skin and circulation, as well as a stronger immune system and a general feeling of wellbeing.

As Hippocrates said: 'There is a remedy for every illness to be found in nature.' This is certainly true of the oils and the ways in which they can assist. Medically, they can assist with acute and chronic illness as well as heightening the body's ability to cope with stress; they can also prevent infection because of the natural antiseptic properties contained in them. They can be used to stimulate or calm the nervous system; some protect the body from illness; some speed up wound-healing; some help detoxify the system; some counteract viral and fungal infections with their antibiotic and anti-viral properties.

Chapter 9 consists of an index of complaints, conditions and minor disorders that the oils can treat. They range from stress-related problems to skin care, from women's complaints to help with colds, flu and sinusitis.

How do you use or apply the oils?

There are five main ways: massage, aromatic baths, inhalation, compresses and vaporization.

Massage: The application of the oils through massage is the most common method, as the oil enters the body through contact with every part of the skin. It is an extremely relaxing and reassuring experience. When using the oils for massage, always dilute them in a vegetable base oil. This is because they are extremely concentrated in their undiluted form, and if applied straight to the skin can sting, burn and cause severe irritation. There are several types of massage: Swedish, acupressure and shiatsu are just a few. Depending on the school at which an aromatherapist trained, she will use one or all of the different methods.

In order to obtain maximum benefit from the oils, it is best to leave them on for six to eight hours so that they can be totally absorbed into the system. It is therefore a good idea to bath before a treatment rather than afterwards.

Aromatic baths: The nerve endings of the skin are an extension of the limbic portion of the brain, which is the area responsible for feelings of pleasure, wellbeing and contentment as well as appetite, thirst and sexual behaviour. A good soak in a scented bath to which a few drops of essential oil have been added can soothe and revitalize.

Inhalation: This method is particularly useful for colds, flu or any condition that brings about congestion in the nose, head or chest. Simply add a few drops of the appropriate oil to a bowl of boiling water; when the water has slightly cooled, inhale the fumes. Alternatively you can put a few drops of oil on a tissue and inhale the scent whenever you choose.

Compresses: This method is very comforting and soothing for aches, strains and cramps. A compress can be made from a piece of cotton gauze or a handkerchief. Fill a bowl with hot water, add a few drops of the oil, soak the fabric in the liquid and apply it to the appropriate areas, which can then be further covered with hot towels. The compress can be left for ten or fifteen minutes, and can be hot or cold depending on the requirement. Heat helps absorption and can be very reassuring.

Vaporization: The oils can be used to perfume or disinfect a room in a number of ways:

1. Put a few drops on a light bulb. The heat will release the scent.

2. Place a few drops on a radiator or in a bowl of water near a radiator. At night, this can help you sleep or help clear a stuffy head, depending on the oil chosen.

3. Some shops now sell oil burners with a small shelf for

the oil and a small night candle which is burnt underneath.

4. The oil can be added to a water spray and sprayed in a room.

How long do the oils last?

Once you have bought your oils, there are several points to remember to ensure they last as long as possible.

1. Store them in a cool place away from strong light. You can use the fridge, but if you do the oils can thicken and not pour easily until warmed, which can be done by simply holding the bottles in your hands for a few minutes.

2. Store them in dark *glass* bottles. One lady I know put some sandalwood in a plastic container in her handbag and then took a long train journey. By the time she had got home, the sandalwood had seeped through the plastic all over her bag. The oils are very potent substances and will eventually eat their way through plastic.

3. Keep them well labelled. At the beginning, before you can distinguish the various scents by smell, it is easy to get the bottles confused. Remember that the bottles can get oily and their labels can therefore slip off. Clean your bottles regularly and use easy-to-read labels, so that you don't end up sniffing at a bottle and thinking 'Now, just *what* is that?'

4. The oils are affected by light, heat, oxygen and moisture, so always replace the tops to maintain quality. If kept properly, most of the oils will last up to a year. You can usually tell if they have 'gone off' as they will smell rancid.

How do I mix the oils?

Mixing the oils is an art in itself. In the early days, when you are experimenting, you will find yourself mixing some curious concoctions and, although maybe they will be therapeutically sound, they may smell pretty odd. Trial, error and a sensitive nose should bring the right results.

Sometimes one oil is quite sufficient, so don't feel you have to mix a blend. If you do, however, don't use more than three oils (more would confuse the system and cancel out the good effects). Remember that the oils will only dissolve in either oil or alcohol.

The quantities given below are approximations, as every case is different. They are given as a guideline for safe use and will be fine if you do not exceed them except on a practitioner's advice.

For children always halve the dosage, as they are more sensitive to the oils than adults.

For massage: As mentioned before, in its concentrated form the oil can sting or burn if applied directly to the skin, so for massage the first thing you will need is a 'carrier oil' to dilute it. Use a vegetable oil rather than baby oil or oil containing lanolin; vegetable oil penetrates the skin best while lanolin is not absorbed and irritates some sensitive skins. Try and obtain a vegetable oil that is pure, unrefined and cold-pressed. Examples are wheatgerm (very rich, but good for dry skin), apricot and peach kernel (both light, and therefore good choices for the face), jojoba, avocado (good for dry skin), almond, grapeseed (excellent, as it is light and easily absorbed), sunflower, soya and olive (although some people do not like the smell of olive oil). These oils are available at most good health shops or stores such as Body Shop. If you are buying a combination massage oil made up from different oils, check (for the reason given above) that one of the components is not lanolin.

Put enough vegetable oil to cover your whole body in a small pot (obviously this is going to differ from size to size and skin to skin but normally 1 tablespoon of base oil). Usually, four to six drops of essential oil in a vegetable base oil are enough for a massage. So for a mixture of three essential oils, add two drops of each into your base. For a mixture of two essential oils, add two drops of each to the base. And for a single essential oil, put four to six drops with the base.

This may not seem like a lot of the actual essential oil – but believe me, it is enough. Recent studies on the potency of the oils showed that one single drop of galbanum added to an Olympic-sized swimming pool could be detected by a faint earthy aroma! It is not true that the more you use, the more effective is the treatment. In fact, sometimes the *less* you use the more effective it is. For example, if you use too much peppermint it can irritate, whereas if you use just the right amount it will relieve.

For baths: Usually, in an average-size bath, four to six drops of essential oil are enough.

For inhalations: Four to five drops in hot water are sufficient.

For compresses: The amount of oil needed for compresses obviously depends on the area to be covered. As a guide, six to eight drops diluted in the water in which the compress is then soaked are usually enough.

For a pleasing scent: There are three notes in scent: top, middle and base. Top is the first that hits you and is the highest, sweetest and most uplifting. It is also the quickest to evaporate. Middle is more moderate, whilst base is the heaviest, slowest and most lingering. It can hold back powerful top notes and is often quite sedative. A combination of the three usually makes a good blend, as too much top can be too intense, light and heady whilst too much base can be too pungent.

Some oils, such as peppermint or clove, can totally overpower a mix. Lemon and lavender are good neutralizers for 'aroma disasters'.

The spices always blend with the spices, the fruits with the fruits and the flowers with the flowers but to restrict oneself to these combinations would be limiting the perfume potential. Sometimes, when people are unwell, they may be intuitively attracted to the oil which is going to help them through their illness. Later, however, when they have recovered, the smell of that particular oil may not seem quite so attractive because their needs have changed. So one way of choosing the correct oil is – whilst keeping in mind the therapeutic qualities – to let the person to be treated sample the aroma of a few oils and choose the one they find most attractive at that particular time. The aroma is an important part of the treatment, so if someone does not like a particular smell another can often be found with similar properties but with a different scent.

The right dilution is also important. In concentrated form the oils can be overpowering, but with the right dilution they can be wonderful. Usually, one drop to 10–20 ml of base oil will give an identifying aroma.

Can I take the oils by mouth?

This is the normal method used by many aromatherapists in France, where practitioners are thoroughly trained; in the UK, however, many aromatherapists are not so sure and warn against possible reactions. The wrong amount can have a harmful effect and irritate or damage the stomach lining.

Actually, in most cases, the oral method is not necessary, as massage is quite adequate to get the oils into the system. The same amount of essential oil finds its way into the bloodstream whether taken orally or massaged in – although some practitioners would argue that the oral method is particularly good for digestive and urinary complaints.

I would not recommend anyone to take the oils orally without having been prescribed to do so by a fully qualified aromatherapist.

Are there any dangers, or times when the oils shouldn't be used?

As mentioned earlier, don't use the oils in their concentrated state directly on the body, because they can irritate the skin. I know of one lady who read that eucalyptus oil was good for clearing the sinuses, so she liberally applied it to her face. Her face stung and then came out in red patches which lasted for days. If she had put a few drops in hot water and inhaled the fumes, she would have had far better results.

Never put the oils in your eyes or on the surrounding sensitive tissue.

The following oils should be avoided altogether as they can severely disturb the system: mugwort, thuja, mustard, wormseed, pennyroyal and sassagras. They are in any case not generally available.

Certain oils – sage, cinnamon, clove, ginger and peppermint – can irritate the skin even in a bath. The following are also best avoided by people with particularly sensitive skins: basil, fennel, lemon grass, rosemary and verbena. If you know your skin is sensitive, start with a quarter of the recommended amount of oil and slowly build from there, all the time watching for any reaction.

During pregnancy, avoid pennyroyal, basil, clove, hyssop, myrrh, cypress, cinnamon, savoy, thyme, origamum, jasmine, rose, marjoram, clary-sage, juniper and sage. (see also Chapter 5.) Additionally, in the first three months fennel, peppermint and rosemary should be avoided.

People who suffer from epilepsy should avoid sage, fennel, hyssop, wormwood and rosemary oils. They can induce a fit if the wrong quantity is used.

The oils should not be used if you have a serious complaint. Don't try and self-diagnose or think it will just go away. Seek professional help, and then see if aromatherapy is an appropriate part of your recovery programme. Aromatherapists are not doctors.

Don't have treatment if you are suffering from meningitis, hepatitis, Parkinson's disease, diptheria or cancer, unless aromatherapy is specifically recommended by a doctor who has a clear knowledge of how it works.

If you are taking homeopathic medicines, check with your homeopath that you can use the oils as some of them interfere with homeopathic remedies.

Where do I get the oils from?

There are no short cuts to quality in essential oils, and in order to ensure you are getting the best and purest you should buy from an established, recommended supplier rather than go for a bargain offer elsewhere. See p. 127 for the addresses of recommended suppliers, many of whom operate a mail order service. Alternatively you could ask local aromatherapists for advice, as they will only use suppliers they can guarantee.

As aromatherapy becomes more and more popular, I have no doubt that many oils will be sold as 'aromatherapy' oils or 'essential' oil. However, closer inspection will reveal that the bottle contains only a few drops of the actual aromatherapy oil mixed with different dilutants.

Price is usually the giveaway. If, for example, rose or neroli are being sold at the same price as lavender, then you know it's not pure oil. Rose, jasmine and neroli are always the most expensive – sometimes as much as six or seven times more expensive than more easily obtainable oils. For instance, 100 kg of rose gives just 1/2 litre of oil, whereas 100 kg of eucalyptus can give 10 litres of oil. Prices may vary (as do purity and scent) from year to year, as crops, harvest, country of origin, weather and the time of picking must be taken into consideration. For example, sandalwood from Mysore is twice the price of Australian (and usually much better), and Moroccan jasmine is often better and costlier than Chinese. Rather like choosing a good wine, it doesn't hurt to consult an expert; a good supplier will be in touch with the rise and fall and different seasons in oil quality.

Another good tip is to familiarize yourself with a guaranteed supplier's price list. Use it as a guideline when out purchasing. If you see that frankincense is cheaper than lavender and on your price list it is three times as expensive, you'll know something's up.

As you become familiar with the oils another giveaway will present itself, and that is the colour (whether rich or transparent) and smell. The more you work with the oils the more sensitive your sense of smell will become, and soon you'll be able to detect a good-quality oil from a more insipid variety by a simple sniff.

Aromatherapy is called a holistic treatment – what does this mean?

The term 'holistic' is derived from the Greek word *holos*, meaning whole. A holistic treatment is one that considers the whole person, not just the injured or diseased part. A holistic practitioner will look at a client's lifestyle, diet, medical history, and mental, emotional and physical state before attempting treatment. As Plato said, 'The cure of the part should not be attempted without the treatment of the whole.' A holistic practitioner will look for the root of the complaint and try to treat that, so that the symptom will not only disappear, but not recur.

For instance, if you have a headache you can either take a pill or you can ask why you got the headache in the first place – was it stress (a mental build-up), or was it physical (perhaps strained shoulders and neck from carrying heavy shopping, or bad posture)? Or perhaps the reason was diet – an allergy or build-up of toxins in the body; some people find that sugar and coffee, for example, can give them a headache. If the root is uncovered then recovery can be permanent; but if only the symptom is treated, relief is just temporary.

Although the holistic approach is not always the most short-term treatment, it is the most thorough and beneficial. People these days often live fast lifestyles, especially in the big cities, and they want fast solutions to ailments. Indeed drugs and pills can be very effective when the pain has gone too far (although sometimes they can have strong side-effects), but prevention in the first place is the best method.

In ancient times, people visited a physician when they were well to keep their system in balance and harmony. If they became ill and the physician hadn't forseen it, they didn't pay the bill! Similarly, holistic treatment these days would be best if taken regularly. In this way the body would always be kept in optimum condition and minor complaints would never be allowed to build up to something major.

How can I find an aromatherapist, and what should I expect if I went for aromatherapy treatment?

Today, many people claim to be aromatherapists without having undertaken proper training. A knowledge of massage and a few of the essential oils isn't enough to qualify. But don't be alarmed: there are now several aromatherapy schools that offer thorough and proficient training. For a list of trained practitioners in your area write to the address listed on p. 128.

Two aromatherapists who have undergone the same training can give very different treatments. Some are very gentle, while others work more deeply. Some qualify in other areas of body work, for example shiatsu, reflexology or polarity therapy, as an extension of their work. It's important for you to feel comfortable with your practitioner as a person and also with their particular touch. Try a few different ones until you find one with whom you feel confident. Recommendation from people you know is a good sign.

A trained aromatherapist will always mix up individual blends for particular clients. Some salons that claim to do aromatherapy buy ready-mixed blends (one for cellulite, one for relaxing, one for revitalizing and so on); although these establishments give a pleasant massage with the oils, they cannot claim to have made up a mixture with one unique individual's requirements in mind. This is part of the magic of true aromatherapy – the blending to someone's needs at one particular moment in time, and the ability to change to another more appropriate blend as the mood alters.

Although both men and women become aromatherapists the majority at present are women, so from now on I will refer to the aromatherapist as 'she'. On your first visit she will probably ask you questions and take a record of your medical history, the reason you have sought treatment, your lifestyle, diet and general state of health and mind. This is to help the aromatherapist decide which oils are going to help you the most, so the more you communicate the more she can help you. She may suggest a series of treatments as part of a programme for you, and may give general advice about diet and lifestyles to assist you further.

Usually she will ask you to remove most of your clothing and lie on the couch. Then she will cover you with towels and prepare the blend of oils ready for a body massage. Depending on the condition to be treated, she may also use compresses or inhalations.

As mentioned before, every practitioner has her own touch. If someone is going too hard or too gently for you, say so; everyone's sensitivity level is different, and between you you can work out what feels best. Also say if you don't like the scent of the oils she has mixed. Quite often a different-smelling blend can be made which will be equally therapeutic.

During the treatment, don't feel you have to make conversation. It's your hour and you'll probably benefit much more if you keep quiet, relax and surrender to the soothing touch and scent.

After the massage, you'll probably be left to get up and dress in your own time. Then your aromatherapist may recommend further treatment or make you a blend to use at home.

Try to organize your treatments so that you have time to relax afterwards. If you go straight back into a busy schedule, part of the benefit can be undone. Some of my clients like to go home and sleep (that is, if they haven't already done so on the couch!).

You should leave the oils on for six to eight hours to ensure maximum absorption. It is best, therefore, to bath beforehand and arrive clean and free of perfume or scent, as these can interfere with the oil's aromas.

Sometimes people get a slight reaction after treatment – usually the first, if they have never had any kind of body work done before or if their system is particularly congested. The reaction can take the form of a mild headache, or a short period of feeling a bit 'fluey' or tired. These symptoms won't last and are usually a good sign – the body is cleansing itself of waste. If the symptoms persist or any questions arise, call the aromatherapist.

Whether you are having a complaint treated or not, it is a good idea to have regular treatments as a way of keeping healthy and holding stress at arm's length.

Different aromatherapists and their books seem to contradict each other about which oil is best for different conditions. Why?

These contradictions are often confusing to newcomers to aromatherapy. For example, one aromatherapist may recommend eucalyptus for a bad chest and the next book make no mention of it but heartily recommend pine, leaving the reader wondering – which is best? Actually the answer would be that either oil is perfectly appropriate. More often than not the books aren't contradicting each other but have emphasized one oil to select without mentioning the others. Usually this is just a personal choice on the part of the author.

I am sure that if I asked four different aromatherapists to select oils and indicate the conditions for which they used them (as I have in Chapter 8), I would get four different lists. This doesn't mean that those oils not mentioned are less potent. It is just a question of individual preference. When you get familiar with the oils, you will have your favourites as well.

This is part of the joy and magic of aromatherapy. Two cooks would never agree totally on how to use their ingredients, and two painters using the same basic colours will create different paintings. Aromatherapy is an art also – for each individual in each different time and mood there is an appropriate oil. Through sensitivity and experience and a thorough knowledge of the basic guidelines you can learn to select the ones that are most beneficial therapeutically and most pleasing to your nose.

AT HOME WITH AROMATHERAPY

The average Westerner's bathroom cabinet contains a number of similar remedies for flu, colds, stomach upsets, hangovers, constipation and suchlike – everyday ailments that are an accepted part of twentieth-century living. In this chapter I would like to recommend the twelve oils that I think will be most useful to deal with these common complaints, as natural alternatives to the chemist's pills and potions.

Newcomers to aromatherapy often complain that there are so many oils which all seem to have so many uses, and they don't know which ones would be of most practical use in the home. Those mentioned here will make an excellent 'starter kit' and provide maximum benefit, as they can be used on their own or in combination with one of the others as shown at the end of the chapter.

BASIC KIT

Basil	Peppermint
Bergamot	Rose
Camomile	Rosemary
Eucalyptus	Sandalwood
Juniper	Tea-tree
Lavender	Ylang-ylang

BASIL

Countries of origin: France, USA, Madagascar, India, the Seychelles, Réunion.
Part of plant from which oil obtained: Whole plant.
Method of extraction: Distillation.
Uses: As a nerve tonic, also for respiratory complaints, gout, loss of concentration, mental fatigue, warts, snakebite, fainting, insomnia, difficult periods, headaches, migraine.
Properties: Antiseptic, anti-spasmodic, tonic, expectorant, emmenagogue (encourages menstrual flow).
Particularly useful for: Pre-exam, studying, meetings.

Derived from the Greek word *basilican*, meaning a royal remedy, basil is just that with its marvellous head-clearing ability and clean smell. The main reason why I have chosen to include it as one of my twelve basic oils is its value in counteracting mental fatigue. Basil doesn't just wake you up – it can also sharpen the memory and aid concentration. After periods of intense study at school or at work one's mind can get bogged down with facts, theories and opinions to the point where it goes blank and can't think straight any more. Pre-exam or pre-presentation this can be unnerving, to say the least. Basil to the rescue! It will revive a weary brain, enabling you to think things through again, giving your mind clarity and renewed strength. The brain, like all our muscles, can seize up if overworked and needs a little attention.

There are various ways in which it can be used. Try putting a little neat oil on a tissue; then bring it out during the meeting or exam and inhale it.

Alternatively ask a family member to mix a few drops in a vegetable base oil and give you a short head-and-neck rub. (Even just five minutes will help.) Ask them to use gentle strokes over the temple, forehead and back of the neck. This could be done regularly throughout the studying or just before the event (exam, deadline or presentation) to give your brain renewed clarity.

Have regular basil baths, with four to six drops in the bathwater. Get in and relax, breathing deeply.

BERGAMOT

Countries of origin: Morocco, West Africa, Italy, Guinea.
Part of plant from which oil is obtained: Peel of nearly-ripe fruit.
Method of extraction: Cold pressing.
Uses: Uplifting, stress, digestion, skin problems, urinary complaints, also as a tonic.
Properties: Antibiotic, antiseptic, diuretic.
Particularly useful for: Acne, depression, cystitis.
Important: Bergamot was used in the past in certain tanning lotions because of its ability to promote a tan; but no longer. In sun or ultra-violet light it can cause abnormal pigmentation of the skin, so beware of using it on your skin if you are going out into the sunlight.

Everyone has days when they are feeling a bit low. A bath with bergamot is just the remedy to banish the clouds and refresh you, so that you feel like facing the day.

It is also a 'must' for teenagers with troubled skin or acne. Either use it with other oils as recommended in Chapter 4, or apply weekly in a compress, leaving it on the skin for five to ten minutes. A compress can be made simply from a thin cotton handkerchief or a piece of gauze. Fill a bowl with hot water, add four to six drops of bergamot, soak the compress in the water, let it cool to body temperature and cover the face. It could not be easier for teenagers, who very often cannot be bothered with fussy routines, and is an excellent remedy for what can be an embarrassing and frustrating condition.

Bergamot is also one of the main oils used for help with

urinary complaints. Either put four drops in a sitz bath and soak for ten minutes, or buy a douche from any chemist and add a couple of drops to the warm water used. It will bring great relief, especially for cystitis. For more effective relief for this condition, it can be used in combination with other oils from the list of twelve.

CAMOMILE

Countries of origin: France, Hungary, Yugoslavia, Britain, North Africa.
Part of plant from which oil is obtained: Flowers, leaves.
Method of extraction: Distillation.
Uses: A calming sedative; used for menstrual problems, irritation (mental and physical), migraine, poor digestion, conjunctivitis. Soothes inflamed skin conditions such as eczema, allergies, herpes, psoriasis, acne, sores, burns, bites, dermatitis.
Properties: Antiseptic, anti-bacterial, anti-inflammatory, sedative, antibiotic, anti-viral, diuretic, analgesic. You may find two types of camomile on sale. German camomile which is quite mild and Roman which is much stronger.
Particularly useful for: Agitated children, and any kind of irritation. Sore stomachs.

This is the ideal oil for the end of the day if you have got overtired children. Try a few drops in their evening bath to help calm them down ready for the night's sleep. As a gentle sedative it helps soothe frayed nerves. Since it is an oil that deals with both physical and mental irritation, it is a valuable choice for the kit. Basically camomile is a good general oil to have in the home for any situation requiring a soothing, gentle balm.

My mother used to suffer from eczema on one leg which caused her much discomfort because of the itchiness. With the help of camomile the irritation was calmed. I simply gave her a massage oil made from a base of grapeseed containing lavender and camomile, and asked her to rub it in every evening.

As a painkiller it is handy to have around for headaches, toothache, stomach ache and menstrual pains; camomile will always lessen the intensity of pain. It can be applied with a base oil in a gentle massage to add relief, or applied in a compress for ten minutes. For period pains it is particularly comforting to apply a warm compress to the lower back and abdomen and to cover the area with a heated towel.

EUCALYPTUS

Countries of origin: Southern Europe, North Africa, Australia.
Part of plant from which oil is obtained: Leaves, twigs.
Method of extraction: Distillation.
Uses: Respiratory: coughs, cold, sore throats, sinusitis. Also for rheumatism, fever, cuts, burns, strained muscles, herpes, cystitis, fungal infection and as a mosquito repellent.
Properties: Antiseptic, expectorant, anti-spasmodic, disinfectant, stimulant, anti-viral, anti-bacterial.
Particularly useful for: Rheumatic and respiratory conditions, muscle strain, purifying the atmosphere.
Important: Don't put eucalyptus on the face undiluted. It will really sting and cause redness.

This oil is particularly useful in winter, when the family is coming home with blocked noses and coughs and colds. It is wonderful for clearing congestion in the respiratory tract and for disinfecting the atmosphere. It can be used in several ways.

As eucalyptus is anti-viral and anti-bacterial, in order to prevent germs spreading and to help the sufferer breathe more easily put a few drops in some water by a bedroom radiator before going to sleep. The scent will permeate the air during the night, making breathing easier and protecting anyone coming near.

Alternatively, put a few drops in boiling water in a bowl. Let it cool a little, then breathe in the aroma while covering your head and face with a towel. Uncover your head when you need to, then repeat. This is marvellous for a blocked nose and stuffy head.

For a massage, put a few drops in some base oil and rub it in around the chest, neck and head area. To clear the sinus apply gentle pressure with the thumb or index finger a) along the eyebrow line b) from the nose crease along the cheekbone, and then repeat from the inner brow to the side of the nostril along the cheek curve. This can bring considerable relief, and often people find they can breathe again after being blocked up.

Eucalyptus is also wonderful for muscular aches and can be used in the bath or applied with base oil to the strained part of the body.

JUNIPER

Countries of origin: Southern Europe, Canada, USA, North Africa, Northern Asia.
Part of plant from which oil is obtained: Berries.
Method of extraction: Distillation.
Uses: Liver problems, cystitis, urinary infections, acne, skin problems, eczema, psoriasis, obesity, gout, difficult periods, flatulence, and as a tonic and blood purifier.
Properties: Detoxifying, diuretic.
Particularly useful for: Hangovers, slimming and cleansing.

After a night on the town, nothing could be better than a morning bath or massage with a few drops of juniper. It will help clear the liver and body of toxins. As juniper is also a diuretic, to assist the cleansing process drink as much water as possible. With regular use, diluted in a vegetable base oil, it can help sufferers of arthritis and rheumatism.

LAVENDER

Countries of origin: France, Italy, Britain, Yugoslavia, Tasmania.
Part of plant from which oil is obtained: Flowering tops.
Method of extraction: Distillation.
Uses: Aches and pains in general, rheumatics, headaches, insomnia, cystitis, high blood pressure, skin problems (bites, burns, eczema, acne, boils, sunstroke and sunburn), paralysis, bronchitis, migraine, palpitations, coughs, colds, stomach upsets. Also to regulate the nervous system, to aid relaxation and as an air purifier.
Properties: Analgesic, anti-convulsive, anti-depressant; helps skin cells regenerate.
Particularly useful for: Burns, stress, insomnia.

If you could only have one oil, I would recommend lavender. As you can see from its uses and properties, it is a great all-rounder. The name is derived from the Latin *lavare*, to wash, and its clean, light smell is liked by most people.

For relaxation add a few drops to your bathwater at night. Alternatively a few drops in some massage oil applied to the body will help undo the tensions of the day. You can feel the tension start to float away as the oil is absorbed into the bloodstream and begins to work on the nervous system, unwinding and relaxing.

If a headache is caused by stress, the soothing effect of lavender will help tense muscles relax. For a partner who comes home from a demanding day, it is wonderful to be given a gentle neck-and-head massage with this oil. It really can change one's mood.

Some people who have trouble sleeping put a few drops of lavender on their pillow. I always keep a bottle by my bed, and if ever I have a lot on my mind and my sleep is disturbed I inhale the scent. Usually I fall back asleep in minutes. Try this oil for children who cannot settle down to sleep. Sprinkle a little on their nightclothes, or put a drop in their evening bath. (Remember, always use half the normal amount of essential oil for children.)

Children also often come home with cuts, burns, bruises and bites. Lavender is a natural antiseptic, and one of the few oils that can be used neat on the skin. Apply the oil to a cotton bud or cotton wool and treat the injured or infected area. It is particularly soothing for burns, possibly because of its ability to help skin cells regenerate, and quickens the whole healing process.

Dr Jean Valnet marvelled at lavender's ability to heal, and told the story of a friend who was cynical about it. The man purposely burnt two fingers. One he bathed in lavender, the other he left. The next day, the first finger had healed up whilst the other was still inflamed and sore.

PEPPERMINT

Countries of origin: All over the world, but mainly USA, Europe, China.
Part of plant from which oil is obtained: Whole plant.
Method of extraction: Distillation.
Uses: Respiratory conditions, fainting, halitosis, nausea, travel sickness, vomiting, headaches, migraine, liver problems, painful periods, sweaty feet, flatulence and as a mosquito repellent.
Properties: Stimulant.
Particularly useful for: Headaches (especially when accompanied by nausea) or for freshening effect.

Peppermint oil has many uses, as you can see. It contains menthol, which is familiar to many for its refreshing scent.

Before a journey, make sure you have some peppermint in the car. If someone is feeling nauseous open the windows, put a few drops of the oil on a tissue and ask them to inhale. It is marvellous for calming a churning stomach.

Try this simple treatment for a throbbing headache. Fold a small towel, into a strip small enough to cover the forehead. Put some cold water and a few drops of peppermint oil in a bowl. Soak the towel, then wring it out and refold it as before. Lie down on a firm surface (the floor with a blanket on top will do). Apply the cold towel to the forehead and lean on either side for six to eight seconds, applying pressure to the head. Then lift the towel. You will be surprised at how much heat gets transmitted to the cool towel. Now lift the head and put the towel round the back of the neck. Lift and pull very gently. This can bring considerable relief to the aching head. You may wish to lie a while with the cold compress on your forehead.

For aching, hot feet peppermint is a wonderfully cooling oil. After a day on your feet put a few drops in a foot bath and soak for ten minutes.

ROSE

Countries of origin: Bulgaria, France, Morocco, Turkey, USSR.
Part of plant from which oil is obtained: Flowers.
Method of extraction: Enfleurage.
Uses: PMT, grief, menopause, skin care, psychic disorders, constipation, and as a heart tonic and aphrodisiac.
Properties: Anti-depressant, antiseptic, aphrodisiac.
Particularly useful for: Frigidity, deep grief, dry and ageing skin, and for its fragrance.

Although rose oil is expensive, it is well worth investing in. Known as the queen of the oils, its aroma and healing properties can assist with many emotional as well as physical upsets. It could be compared to the queen piece in chess, in that it is capable of being used in many different directions.

The ancient Romans used rose oil in their feasts, and in fact it does help the digestion, particularly the liver, if one has been over-indulging. It soothes and cleanses and can help if you are constipated (although there are other less expensive oils that can do the same job).

In any lifetime there are ups and downs, joys and sorrows. Often the lows are hard to bear, especially if they involve the death of a loved one, the loss of a partner through a failed relationship, or unrequited love. It is easy to go to a doctor and say, 'My leg hurts, help me!' But to whom can you go and say, 'My heart is broken. It hurts. I feel empty.'?

This is where rose oil comes into its own. Through gentle massage it can quietly enter the system and go about its work, soothing, healing and lifting the agony of remorse or loss. Apart from its healing properties, the pure aroma of a garden smelling of roses cannot fail to uplift even the saddest soul for a moment.

Touch can be more reassuring than words at these times – in fact silence is probably welcomed. A slow, relaxing massage with rose oil is one of the real gifts you can give someone in emotional pain.

One male client of mine lost his wife just before I started to treat him. At first he was so tense it was more like massaging a suit of armour, but slowly, with the aid of rose oil, over the weeks he started to relax. Later he told me that, when everyone around him was trying to help with consolation and advice on how to deal with the situation, it was only during the aromatherapy treatments that he felt any solace or peace of mind.

The other well-kept secret of rose oil is its use in skin

care. Look at the texture of a rose petal, and imagine what the oil could do for your skin! It is wonderful for sensitive and ageing skins in particular, but any type can benefit from its application (see recipes in Chapter 4).

ROSEMARY

Countries of origin: Spain, France, Yugoslavia, USA, North Africa, Japan, Turkey.
Part of plant from which oil is obtained: Flowers, leaves.
Method of extraction: Distillation.
Uses: Sprains, hair care, flatulence, stomach problems, respiratory complaints, muscular aches and pains, liver trouble, fatigue.
Properties: Tonic, decongestant, astringent, diuretic and stimulant.
Particularly useful for: Stimulating a tired system, dealing with sports strains, and as a hair tonic and diuretic.

As lavender could be called an evening oil because of its ability to relax, so rosemary might be called a morning oil for its ability to awaken. It is stimulating for the system and can banish fatigue and lethargy as well as clearing your head. Put a few drops in your morning bath for a positive start to the day or week. Try it on a Monday morning when no one feels like work or school after the weekend.

Another of the common uses of rosemary is for muscle strain caused by physical fatigue, especially after demanding sports or exercise. After physical exertion massage the affected limbs with base oil containing a few drops of rosemary, or sink into an aromatic bath containing four or five drops of rosemary oil. It is also often used in combination with other oils for rheumatism.

SANDALWOOD

Countries of origin: India, Indonesia.
Part of plant from which oil is obtained: Wood. A tree must be at least thirty years old before the oil can be obtained from it.
Method of extraction: Distillation.
Uses: Urinary problems, cystitis, water retention, respiratory problems, sore throat, stress, frigidity, skin care.
Properties: Antiseptic, anti-spasmodic, diuretic, sedative, aphrodisiac, mild astringent.
Particularly good for: Dry skin, eczema, cystitis, sore throats; also its calming effect and fragrance.

Sandalwood is a powerful antiseptic and can be used effectively for most infections. It is particularly helpful to the respiratory tract, where its anti-spasmodic properties help calm and soothe, and to the urinary area, where it can be applied in a douche or put in a sitz bath.

It is a good oil for men, who seem to prefer its woody fragrance to some of the more flowery alternatives. In fact it is often one of the ingredients used as a fixative in men's perfumes and cosmetics. Sandalwood is also often used in skin care preparations on account of its ability to nourish dry skin and to act as an antiseptic in cases of acne or irritated skin.

TEA-TREE

Countries of origin: Australia.
Part of plant from which oil is obtained: Leaves, twigs.
Method of extraction: Distillation.
Uses: Fungal infections, viral and bacterial infections, burns, colds, flu, warts, acne, verrucae, thrush, snakebite and as an insect repellent.
Properties: Antiseptic, antibiotic, anti-fungal, anti-viral.

Particulary good for: Athlete's foot, thrush, cold sores, lice and as a general antiseptic.

Tea-tree is a must in the home because of its use as an antiseptic. It is a great deterrent to infections, being four or five times stronger than most household disinfectants, yet it is still kind to the skin. In the Second World War it was issued in first aid kits to troops fighting in tropical regions, as it can be used to clean and disinfect cuts, wounds, bruises, ulcers, sores, even insect bites and stings. In his book on aromatherapy Robert Tisserand tells an interesting story about a man who was bitten by a male funnel web spider (usually deadly). But the man knew of the potency of the tea-tree and applied the oil from the leaves and twigs to the bite on the way to the hospital. This prompt attention eased the pain and he lived to tell the tale. It is fascinating that the funnel web spider is found in New South Wales, which is just where tea-tree oil comes from – another example of the for-every-nettle-there's-a-dock-leaf idea.

For stings, wounds and skin abrasions put a little neat tea-tree oil on a cotton bud and apply to the area.

For infections of the chest or throat, put a few drops in a base oil and massage into the infected area or apply with a hot compress. This can be particulary comforting for a tight chest or racking cough. (Look for other combinations of oils on p. 111.)

YLANG-YLANG

Countries of origin: Far East.
Part of plant from which oil is obtained: Flowers.
Method of extraction: Distillation.
Uses: High blood pressure (regulates and calms the heart), insect bites. Also relaxes and uplifts, and used for skin and hair care.

Properties: Aphrodisiac, antiseptic, anti-depressant.
Particularly good for: Aphrodisiac, balance, irritability, palpitations, fragrance.

With its light floral scent, ylang-ylang has the ability simply to make you feel good. It is named by most aromatherapists as the most obvious aphrodisiac; its properties enable the nervous system to relax, but instead of sending you to sleep it lifts you, giving you a feeling of lightness and casting irritability a hundred miles away. It is a great oil for making you feel mellow, so I have included it as one to use for special occasions to evoke a mood of wellbeing.

Life is made up not so much of events but rather of our reactions and responses to those events. Two people in the same place at the same time can have totally opposite experiences depending on their state of mind. How many times has a 'planned' good time been a real let-down because, although all the ingredients were there externally, you just couldn't get in the mood because of stress or exhaustion or plain irritation? This is where ylang-ylang comes in. It has a delightful scent and can arouse a real sense of joy to be alive. This is why I have included it in the basic list of twelve oils, although it also has other properties and in combination with other oils is of great practical use in the home.

USING THE OILS IN COMBINATION

Here are some ways you can use the oils listed above in combination. It is only a guide just to give you a start at mixing; as you become more familiar with the oils you will no doubt make your own according to your personal preferences. Remember the basic rules:

1. Don't use more than three oils in one mix.
2. Sometimes one is quite adequate – don't feel you *have* to combine oils.

3. For massage, five or six drops of essential oil in enough vegetable base oil to cover the body is usually adequate. So if you're using three different oils, two drops of each is sufficient.

4. Six drops is usually enough to perfume a bath.

Using the index of oils on p. 97 and the index of minor ailments on p. 111 you can add to your basic kit. For example, I haven't mentioned cinnamon oil in this chapter, yet it is a wonderful oil for warming in winter and for convalescing after illness. It could be used in combination with ylang-ylang for someone who had been ill and needed cheering, or with rosemary in winter for someone who had been out on a football pitch and was tired and cold. Peppermint is also effective in these situations. It is a useful oil on its own, but could be used with camomile to soothe stomach cramps and with lavender to relax, or with rosemary and basil to clear the head and wake you up, or with lavender for headaches, or with eucalyptus for the chest. Get the idea? Keep checking the indexes and the properties – the combinations are almost infinite.

SOME RECIPES FROM THE BASIC KIT OILS

Condition: Waking up (morning)
Oil: Rosemary and bergamot
Method: Bath or massage

Condition: Unwinding (evening)
Oil: Lavender and bergamot
Method: Bath or massage

Condition: Detoxifying for hangovers
Oil: Juniper and rosemary
Method: Bath or massage

Condition: Colds, flu, bad chest

Oil: Eucalyptus, rosemary and lavender, *or* tea-tree,
  sandalwood and eucalyptus
Method: Bath, inhalation or massage

Condition: Sinusitis
Oil: Peppermint, eucalyptus and rosemary
Method: Inhalation

Condition: Special occasion
Oil: Ylang-ylang, sandalwood and rose
Method: Bath or massage

Condition: Overworked and fatigued
Oil: Rosemary and basil
Method: Bath or massage

Condition: Dry skin care
Oil: Sandalwood and rose
Method: In light base oil (or see recipes in Chapter 4)

Condition: Cystitis
Oil: Sandalwood, tea-tree and bergamot
Method: Aromatic bath, compress or douche

Condition: For wounds and burns
Oil: Tea-tree and lavender
Method: Neat on cotton bud or cotton wool

Condition: Refreshing
Oil: Basil and bergamot
Method: Bath/splash

Condition: Travel sickness
Oil: Peppermint and lavender
Method: On tissue

USEFUL TRAVEL KIT OILS

Basil (for the driver, to keep the head clear and concentration focused). Peppermint (for any passengers who get travel-sick). Lavender (to unwind in an aromatic bath at the end of the journey).

The Frankfurt package: These recipes are so-named for my editor, who goes to the Frankfurt Book Fair once a year. She asked what oils would be useful to take.

1. Rosemary and bergamot for the bath, for a refreshing start to the day after inevitable late nights.

2. Basil and bergamot for the daytime, to clear the head and conquer mental fatigue. A few drops can be put on a tissue and drawn out to inhale when one's concentration is flagging.

3. Lavender to help unwind at night, and to help switch off and sleep after a demanding day.

AROMATHERAPY AND STRESS

Eighty per cent of my clients come to me because of stress. Sometimes they are aware that they need to unwind and relax, and find aromatherapy a pleasurable way to do so. Sometimes the stress is actually manifesting itself in physical symptoms – for example migraine, insomnia or indigestion, all of which can cause acute discomfort and prevent them from functioning properly.

Either way, aromatherapy can be extremely beneficial in alleviating tension, but it is also important to look into the causes of the stress in the first place. In an age when it is becoming evident that many diseases, from headaches to heart problems, are caused primarily by mental and emotional states that are not dealt with or released in any way, stress should not be simply brushed aside as something that one just has to live with, nor should aromatherapy be overlooked as one of the most effective ways of reducing and dealing with it.

Let us look at some of the causes and the unavoidable cycles they can lead to.

PHYSICAL

1. Long hours at work with no time to eat properly (bad diet – quick snacks – lack of proper nourishment) leads to

decreased vitality.

2. Lack of exercise, resulting in stiffness and decreased energy.

3. Tension causing sleeplessness, resulting in fatigue the following day, creating a vicious circle of still more tension and feelings of being unable to cope.

ENVIRONMENTAL

1. Transport: long journeys, delays, rush-hour traffic, overcrowded tubes and buses all add up to stressful situations. A near-miss with an irritated driver may be 'forgotten' by the time you get to work but it gets stored in the body and stress can result. Delays on public transport can make one late, causing tension. Many of my clients travel on the Northern Line on the London Underground and they cite it as one of the major causes of stress with its constant stream of cancellations and delays.

2. Work environment: cramped space, uncomfortable chairs causing bad posture, noise and bad lighting can all be sources of stress.

EMOTIONAL

1. Personal relationships can be a great cause of stress, with divorce ranking number one on the scale. When things are rocky in our private lives, we often have to soldier on with our work and responsibilities in an environment where there is no room for emotional turbulence. Obviously that is going to put an enormous strain on the system, especially if there has been a loss in the family or things are not working out with one's partner.

2. Children at different ages can bring a variety of worries to parents: concern about their schooling, friendships, health, future career and happiness can sometimes cause

great anxiety of a kind that disturbs the normal breathing pattern (as all stress does), resulting in a shallower, sharper breathing.

MENTAL

1. Financial pressures: in these days of rising prices, finances can be the root cause behind the long hours we put in at work and the excessive demands we make upon ourselves simply to stay alive. But to live a life of working in order to eat, and eating in order to work, can wear us down. These demanding situations can increase the flow of adrenalin, which eventually exhausts the system and can so reduce the resilience of the immune system that we become more vulnerable to 'disease'. We know that there is more to life than simply surviving and that we cannot possibly be happy with an unbalanced lifestyle and all that goes with it, such as irritability, resentment and frustration.

2. Job uncertainty: most of us long for security and job satisfaction. Often the two do not go hand in hand and we may have to choose between doing what we want or earning a good living. Of course, some lucky ones have managed to get both. Many of the clients I see are uncertain about which course they should pursue and whether they have the ability, confidence and courage to do what they really want. Should they take a risk? Or should they stay where they are, with the secure and the familiar? A feeling of not being fulfilled can manifest itself as stress because the discontent is sure to find an outlet somewhere, either at work or at home. It is our responsibility to be true to our real needs if we are to avoid setting off a cycle of stress, restlessness and frustration. The result can be bad posture, particularly putting strain on the neck and shoulder areas, leading to headaches or even migraine. Some people hold their tension in their jaw, especially if they are having to hold back what they would

really like to say – they tighten and sometimes grind their teeth at night.

UNSATISFACTORY RELEASE

To relieve the stress, people sometimes turn to alcohol, cigarettes, drugs or overeating. As we know only too well, they all have their price.

1. Cigarettes: bad chest, bad skin, dependency.
2. Alcohol: dependency, hangovers, high blood pressure, bad skin, weight gain.
3. Drugs: dependency, chemical imbalance in the body.
4. Overeating: weight gain, lack of vitality, heart strain.

Sounds pretty miserable, doesn't it? But it need not be so. Aromatherapy can be a vital way of halting these downward spirals. By helping to re-establish balance and harmony in the system, it is the first step to undoing the harm that stress can cause. In addition, it is a completely natural method with only positive after-effects.

Stress is perhaps an inevitable feature of life in the twentieth century. Whatever our age, life will always present us with comings and goings, ups and downs, good and bad times. However, our lives are made up not only of these changing events and circumstances but also of our particular reaction to them. Just notice how, after a good holiday, the traffic or the rush-hour crowds do not frustrate us quite so much; that irritable customer we have to deal with at work does not get to us quite so badly. But a few weeks later, when we are strung out and back in the throes of fast living, it can all seem too much again. State of mind is all-important; balance between body and mind is necessary – but we cannot always be taking holidays or even weekend breaks. Another route people sometimes take is to try to change things externally – redecorate a room, go to the hairdresser's, move house and so on – but ultimately it is internally where real change and true perception and enjoyment of life must come about. This is where aromatherapy treatment can seem like a real life-saver.

TREATMENT FROM A PRACTITIONER

A good aromatherapist will look at your lifestyle and advise you on ways to reduce stress-making conditions. He or she may advise better time management, exercise, diet or even counselling, but the main thing is the treatment which works on the nervous system, so restoring that precious sense of rest and wellbeing. I wish I had a camera to take before-and-after pictures of my clients. Sometimes they arrive fraught, stressed and uptight, and simply collapse on to the couch with a weary sigh. It is amazing how an hour's soothing massage with the right oils can unlock the tensions of the week, encourage tight muscles to let go and generally relax the whole system. Their faces look totally different afterwards – peaceful, 'washed' and often much younger. There is nothing more ageing than stress – weekly aromatherapy sessions help to keep it all at bay.

HOME TREATMENT

Sometimes, for whatever reason, a visit to an aromatherapist is not possible. Maybe she is booked up, or maybe you cannot find a mutually convenient time. You can still benefit enormously with the use of oils at home, in the bath or through massage.

All sorts of stressful situations can present themselves in the home – pre-exam nerves, misunderstandings between family members, job worries and so on. There are oils for all the different circumstances. Many of the essential oils are described as having a relaxing effect, and indeed they do. In this chapter I should like to go into this a little more deeply, as the wonderful thing about the oils is *how* they relax you. They all do it in different ways. Some can relax you to the point where you are ready to sleep. Others will relax and revitalize at the same time. Here is a list of oils that are good for stressful conditions, together with the 'shades' of assistance they offer. So you can choose the one that is just right for you at any particular time.

Basil: Will help revive and clear a weary mind after excess concentration.

Benzoin: Gives a nice, lazy, warm sensation as though you are basking in the warm sun.

Bergamot: Good to use when you are worn out and feeling a bit down, as it is wonderfully uplifting.

Camomile: A calming oil, best used when you are feeling agitated or restless.

Cedarwood: I find all the 'woody' oils very 'grounding'. At those times when you are preoccupied with future plans and events, you can enter into a kind of dream-like state; this is the time when you may become absent-minded, when keys get mislaid, books lost, etc. The 'woods' can bring you back to earth. Cedarwood also gives a sense of reassurance.

Clary-sage: Relaxing to the point of euphoria (not one for when you are already feeling light-headed).

Geranium: The great balancer, can restore a sense of harmony and equilibrium.

Jasmine: A calming serene oil which uplifts, soothes and gives a sense of inner beauty (great if you are feeling old and tired).

Lavender: Relaxing to the point of drowsiness. A good one for late at night when your body is tired but your mind is on overtime, ticking away.

Mandarin: A soothing oil which is particularly good if your stress manifests in a knotted or upset stomach.

Marjoram: A good 'knock-out' oil if you are having difficulty switching off.

Melissa: Works on deep anxiety, helping to chase away black thoughts.

Patchouli: Gives a sense of warmth and friendliness (a nice oil to burn in a room to create a welcoming atmosphere).

Rosemary: Can revive a weary body.

Rose: The great healer, it can give a sense of being 'centred' and made whole again.

Rosewood: Gives a cheering, cosy feeling.

Sandalwood: Can help protect and preserve your energy and give courage to carry on.

Tangerine: A great nerve tonic.

Vetiver: The oil of tranquillity (along with sandalwood, particularly liked by men).

Ylang-ylang: Gives a mellow feeling; it can relax and uplift at the same time.

APPLYING THE OILS

Aromatic baths

Consider how you feel and how you would like to feel. Consult the list of 'stress' oils and choose the appropriate one. On one day, one oil may be enough – in which case, put six to eight drops in your bath. On another day, you may feel a mixture of three is required – in which case two drops of each will be sufficient. Then just lie back and soak it up.

Massage

When you have been overdoing it, nothing is more welcome than a good massage, especially one with the added luxury of the essential oils. The benefits are many: it feels wonderful; it stimulates the circulation; it can relieve pain in joints and muscles; it helps reduce tension; it helps reduce high blood pressure (I once worked above a chemist's shop and the pharmacist often measured clients' blood pressure before and after an aromatherapy session. Invariably, it was lower afterwards.); it can stimulate the immune system; often people sleep more deeply and soundly afterwards (sometimes even during!); and finally it encourages an awareness of tension trapped in the body and its need for release and relaxation.

LEARNING MASSAGE

I thought long and hard about whether to include a section on how to give a massage. Many writers have attempted to do so in the past, but in my opinion this can cause a lot of stress to the reader when trying to follow the instructions. So I decided – since this is a chapter on how to alleviate stress, and I certainly do not want to create any – to omit any such attempt at instruction. I believe that you need to see what to do in order to follow directions clearly. As it is a marvellously useful skill to possess for both long and short massage (a ten-minute massage can completely relieve a headache), my advice would be as follows:

Attend a local massage course

If it is for your own use, you do not have to take a long course involving the study of anatomy and physiology. Often local councils run ongoing courses, and local health shops and clubs are always advertising day-long or weekend workshops. Attending one of these would be far the best method of learning, as you get to watch a massage being given and you get to practise under a trained eye. You will be surprised how much you can pick up in a weekend. You will be taught the main basic strokes:

Effleurage: Long, sweeping movements often used in Swedish massage.

Pettrisage: Kneading movements.

Rubbing
Cupping: Done with the palm of the hand.
Hacking: Done with the sides of the hands.

A teacher can demonstrate the right pressure and show you how to use your body weight. Also you can ask questions if there is something you do not understand.

If you attend the course with a friend or partner, you can practise on each other. Then, when you are more confident, you can massage each other when the need arises.

Of course, if you want to practise professionally, courses are longer and much more thorough (see details on p. 128). But shorter courses for use in the home can be invaluable. The skills you will acquire on one or two weekends will last a lifetime, and there is no doubt that they will be some of the most useful and appreciated skills you could ever bring into the home. (They should teach it at school along with domestic science. In this day and age, anything that combats stress is of great value.)

Learn by having regular treatments

Go to several different practitioners. Everyone has their own style and you can learn from each one. Note the different strokes and the pressure. Watch what they are doing and try it later yourself. It is essential to be on the receiving end when learning, because you experience for yourself what feels good and what doesn't.

Useful tips

Here are some tips for when you have learnt the basics.

1. Go slowly and smoothly. Don't charge in, as there is nothing worse than the feeling that someone is giving you a massage and trying to get it over with. Much of your energy is transferred to the body you are treating. So be still, and take long, deep breaths while you are massaging.

2. Use different speeds, strokes and pressures.

3. Decide the pressure between you. Some people are too polite or shy to say 'Go harder' or 'Go softer'.

4. Create a relaxed and private environment: phones off the hook, TV off, children out of the way. Make sure the room is warm (the body temperature drops significantly when you are lying still being massaged). So have plenty of towels and blankets ready if required.

5. Use soft lighting which is easy on the eye.

6. Pay attention to your posture and bend your knees – not just your back.

7. Use your body weight rather than your muscles. That way, you will not be so exhausted afterwards that you will need a massage yourself in order to recover.

8. In winter, it is a wonderful sensation if the oil has been warmed. So before the massage put it in a small pot on a radiator. Heat can be very reassuring and so, as you work on the body, keep the towels warm on the radiator as well. In this way, those parts of the body which have been treated can be covered with warmth.

9. Warm your hands before starting. There is nothing worse than freezing cold hands being put on one's body.

10. Music sometimes helps people relax, as it distracts them from recurring worries. Do ask what they would like, as some people may prefer it to be quiet. Perhaps ask them to bring their own choice, or to pick something tranquil and conducive to relaxation.

11. Be confident.

4

AROMATHERAPY AND BEAUTY

ESSENTIAL OILS AND YOUR SKIN

The first time I gave my husband a facial with essential oils he could not get over how good his skin looked. Not only that, but the next day he said a number of people at work had asked him what he had been doing to look so good – younger even! How often do we read or hear about serums, potions and lotions at exorbitant prices packaged in glamorous bottles and boxes on which are printed complicated technical theories how they can transform your skin. I have tried a good many myself, but I can honestly say that the only time I really did see a dramatic improvement in my skin was when I started using the essential oils as part of my face routine.

First of all, it is true that beauty comes from within. What we eat and how we live are usually reflected in the condition of our skin, which often resembles a kind of dumping ground for any internal imbalance which manifests itself in spots and pimples. Make-up can only cover up so much, and in fact may simply make matters worse by clogging up an already unhealthy skin.

Some of the causes of a bad or lifeless skin apart from hereditary factors are smoking, alcohol, bad diet (excess sugar, over-refined foods, not enough fresh fruit and vegetables), stress, lack of sleep, illness, lack of exercise and lack of skin care. If any of these apply to you, look into what you can do from the outside. The marvellous thing about the essential oils is that they actually have the ability to penetrate the skin's surface and start working from the inside.

The skin is made up of three layers. At the bottom is the subcutaneous layer, containing muscles and fatty tissue. Next comes the dermis, where blood and lymph vessels, sensory nerves, hair follicles and the sebaceous and sweat glands are located. The sebaceous glands produce sebum, which lubricates the skin and seals moisture into the cells. Sebum also preserves the elasticity of the skin. The sweat glands produce perspiration which escapes through the pores. If these pores are blocked, spots result. The degree of activity of the sebaceous and sweat glands determine whether the skin is dry, greasy or normal. The top layer, made up essentially of dead cells, is called the epidermis. Cells made in the dermis travel up to the top and constantly renew themselves – a process which slows down considerably with age.

As the oils travel right through to the bottom layer, change can come about from within. Skin cells can be fed and nourished by certain oils, whilst other oils are regenerative, stimulating the cell replacement process; still other oils can restore balance if there is under- or over-activity in the sebaceous glands.

DRY SKIN

People with dry skin have under-active sebaceous glands which are unable to produce the oil needed to prevent the skin losing moisture. This can be attributed to a number of factors – illness, sun, use of sunbeds, icy winds, a diet deficient in vital nutrients, alcohol, central heating and antibiotics, to name but a few. After a gentle cleansing and toning, what is needed is to replace the oil not being made and to encourage the glands to function normally again.

To cleanse

This is always an essential step in any face routine, to remove the dust and debris accumulated during the day. Dry skin needs to be treated gently. So choose a mild, unperfumed cleanser, particularly avoiding strongly scented or chemical soaps.

To tone

A camomile, rosewater or rosehip toner is a good base to freshen dry skin. To this you could add a few drops of geranium or ylang-ylang.

It is possible to make a mixture at home very simply. Boil three to four camomile or rosehip teabags in a pint of water, and then leave them to steep. Remove the bags, add a few drops of your essential oil and you have the perfect toner. Make a fresh batch of the mixture every seven to ten days.

To moisturize

While the skin is still moist, apply a moisturizing face oil. This is the most important stage for dry skin. Just slapping on more and more of any old moisturizer is not enough. What is needed is an oil which will get under the surface of the dry, dead skin and down to the dermis, in order to nourish new cells and encourage the sebaceous glands to work normally.

Essential oils

Geranium, rose, sandalwood or neroli (also ylang-ylang and rosewood or patchouli). Do not put the oils straight on to your face, but mix them first in a base oil. Usually 3 per cent essential oil makes an adequate mixture.

Base oils

Jojoba is always a good choice for the skin, as it leaves it with a wonderful satiny feeling and makes an excellent base. Avocado is also good for dry skin because it is so rich. Wheatgerm added to any mixture helps to preserve it. Almond and apricot kernel are also good choices and easily absorbed.

Any of these oils used singly or mixed will be fine for your facial oil. Pick them according to preference. The almond and apricot kernel are lighter oils than the others, but all will dilute the essential oils and be absorbed into the skin.

If you do not want to be bothered mixing up an oil yourself and you have a moisturizer with which you are happy, try adding a little essential oil to it. Mix it well and see if there is any improvement. I am sure there will be! Again, 2–3 per cent essential oil in the base is sufficient.

Weekly treatment

Buy any unperfumed feeding mask for dry skin. Put enough for one treatment in a small pot, then add one drop each of rose, sandalwood and geranium. Apply to the face and leave on according to the directions. The other oils for dry skin – neroli, patchouli, ylang-ylang and rosewood – could also be used in combination.

Alternatively, mix your own from oatmeal, almond oil, water, and three to four drops of essential oil for dry skin. Leave on the face for ten minutes, then remove from the skin and apply your aromatic moisturizer.

GREASY SKIN AND ACNE

This time the sebaceous glands are overactive, producing excess oil. This imbalance can come about through bad diet, such as tea, coffee, fatty or spicy foods and sugar, so all these foods are best avoided. It is also advisable to drink plenty of water and keep to a diet with plenty of fibre and fresh fruit and vegetables.

To cleanse

It is most important to keep greasy skin very clean, or the pores will get clogged with make-up or dust and blackheads or pimples will result. Use a mild, unperfumed cleanser and add a drop of juniper and a drop of lemon. All the oils have antiseptic properties, which help keep bacteria in check and so banish spots and pimples.

To tone

Use either orangewater or a camomile mixture (the same as for dry skin) or a mixture of camomile and witchhazel (witchhazel is a good decongestant). You can use any natural toner without chemicals or perfume. Add to about a pint of your toner two drops of juniper, two drops of bergamot and two drops of lemon.

To moisturize

Often people with greasy skin have an aversion to applying oil, and try to remove all traces of their natural oil, sebum, from the skin. However, any skin actually needs a little oil to protect and lubricate it. To try and remove the oil only starts a vicious circle, as the glands try to produce more to replace what has been lost. Again, what is needed is something to get down to the root of the problem, to rebalance the glands and keep the skin bacteria-free. Certain essential oils will do just this. With time and consistent use the desired results will be achieved, correcting the imbalance and producing long-lasting and noticeable effects as changes come about from within.

Essential oils

Lemon, bergamot, juniper, geranium, sandalwood (geranium

and sandalwood are good for both dry and greasy skin), neroli and lavender (these last two are particularly good if acne has left scarring on the face, as they help to heal blemishes and scars).

Base oils

For this type of skin the finer vegetable oils are usually preferred, such as apricot kernel or peach kernel. Again, 2–3 per cent essential oil will be sufficient. Use the mixture daily.

Weekly treatments

Steaming: To help keep the skin clean and the pores unclogged, boil some water, put it in a bowl and add two drops of juniper, two drops of bergamot and two drops of lavender. Cover your head with a towel and steam your face. Splash your skin with cool water afterwards to close the pores.

Compress: Alternatively, make the mixture in a bowl as above, but this time soak a flannel or gauze in the solution. Place it over your face and leave for ten minutes. Apply a little oil mixture afterwards.

NORMAL SKIN

Even with a good, healthy skin it is a sensible idea to look after it well, starting at an early age.

To cleanse

Use any mild, unperfumed cleanser.

To tone

Use rosewater, camomile or any natural toning water, to which could be added a few drops of ylang-ylang, lavender, neroli or camomile.

To moisturize

Make an oil as before from 3 per cent essential oil and 97 per cent vegetable oil.

Essential oils

Rose, patchouli, geranium, sandalwood, jasmine, ylang-ylang or lemon.

Base oils

Jojoba, apricot, almond or peach kernel make excellent bases.

Weekly treatment

Add three drops of the 'normal skin' essential oils to a natural skin mask, or blend your own mask from fruit (apricots, peaches, apples) or cucumbers. Add three drops of essential oils to the pulp and apply the mixture to your face. Keep on for ten minutes. After removing the pulp, apply a little of your facial moisturizer.

AGEING SKIN

On average, it takes 120 days for new cells in the dermis to move up to the surface and die. This process slows down considerably with age, and the cells are not replaced as frequently. Thus the surface skin can look rather weary. In addition, the elastin fibres and the network of collagen in the dermis, which give the skin its elasticity, slow down and begin to alter. The skin loses its firmness and suppleness.

Face-lifts can stretch and tuck the skin, so reducing wrinkles, but they cannot improve the muscle tone which gives skin its youthful appearance. When someone is under tension, the muscles in the face contract and the skin becomes taut and wrinkled. If the tension is persistent, these lines can become permanent (one has only to look at people's

frown- or laughter-lines). In the end, the habitual express-
ions in your life become etched on your face. It is always a
good idea to deal with stress when it arises and get rid of
tension as soon as possible before it finishes up lining your
face. Early use of the essential oils on your face will help your
skin, but complete, regular aromatherapy treatments will
keep your whole body and system relaxed. It is a good way of
preventing stress from accumulating and becoming a permanent facial feature at too early an age.

Regular use of essential oils cannot remove the years, but
it can certainly help slow down the ageing process. The
sooner you start, the better. The oils encourage the skin to
regenerate, and in feeding it they give it back some of its
vitality.

To cleanse

Use any mild, unperfumed cleanser to remove surface
debris.

To tone

Rosewater or camomile toner are gentle on the skin. Add a
few drops of lavender to the mixture.

To moisturize

This is the most important part of the routine for ageing skin,
which needs to be fed and revitalized. As before, use 3 per
cent essential oil to 97 per cent vegetable base oil.

Essential oils

Rose, neroli, frankincense, myrrh, patchouli, lemon, sandalwood, carrot.

Base oils

Often people with an ageing skin prefer the richer bases (as
for dry skin): wheatgerm, avocado, sesame and jojoba. I find

these work well mixed with the lighter ones such as peach kernel and apricot kernel. Apply your face oil daily, not forgetting your neck.

Weekly treatments

Same as for dry skin, but using the essential oils mentioned here.

Compress: A weekly compress using frankincense, patchouli and rose is excellent for a more mature skin. Boil a pint of water and add two drops of each of the oils. Soak a piece of gauze or flannel. Place it over your face and leave for ten minutes.

Puffy eyes, circles or bags under the eyes are best treated by steeping two camomile teabags in boiling water. Squeeze out excess moisture and, after letting them cool, apply one to each closed eye for five to ten minutes. This is very soothing for tired eyes and can reduce puffiness.

ESSENTIAL OILS AND YOUR BODY

Why not make up an oil for your whole body to nourish your skin all over? You can apply it in any of the following ways:

1. Before getting into a warm bath, cover yourself with oil and then get in and simply soak. The warmth of the bath helps the oil soak into the skin.

2. Put a couple of tablespoons of made-up oil into the bath as you would any bath oil.

3. Put your made-up oil all over your body after your bath. (A word of warning here. Take care not to have too many *hot* baths, as they can dry the skin. It's best to let the water cool a little before you get in.)

Recipes for body oil

You can make up your body oil with 2 per cent essential oil

and 98 per cent base oil. Any of the bases mentioned for the various skin types will be fine. Choose yours according to whether you prefer a richer or a lighter oil and according to your skin type. For the bath and body, it is nice to use a pleasing fragrance combination. Here are some suggestions.

For women: Rose, lavender and sandalwood; jasmine, lemon and patchouli; neroli, lavender and sandalwood; ylang-ylang, lemon and sandalwood; rose, rosewood and geranium.

For men: Lime, lavender and cedarwood.

ESSENTIAL OILS AND YOUR HAIR

Your hair is often the first thing people notice about you, and, as with your skin, it can say so much about you. A good diet and healthy lifestyle will give a healthy head of shiny hair, just as bad diet, illness and stress can make it look lack-lustre and dull. Some people – both men and women – even start losing hair in times of stress.

The way we treat our hair can also damage it. Hair dryers, tints, bleaching, detergent-based shampoos, sun and sea all take their toll on the hair. As with the skin, the first remedy for good hair has to come from within by making any necessary changes in diet or lifestyle. The essential oils, however, can help in treating the hair and restoring it to a good condition as they penetrate the scalp.

Add oils to your usual shampoo and conditioner

Many people cannot be bothered collecting all the ingredients to make up their own totally natural shampoo, but would quite happily add some of the essential oils to commercial products. When buying hair products, bear in mind that some are full of chemicals and some are detergent-based, which does not do the hair any good. It is not always easy to determine the chemical composition of these products as the ingredients are not always stated on the package. But fortunately many health shops stock natural products and have made it their policy to carry only chemical-free stock.

With conditioners, try to buy ones with added protein (keratin and lecithin), as this will help keep your hair healthy.

Essential oils for the hair
Normal: Rosemary, lemon, lavender, cedarwood.
Dry: Sandalwood, camomile, rosemary, lavender.
Greasy: Cypress, lemon, rosemary.

To 100 ml of shampoo or conditioner, add between ten and twelve drops of essential oil.

Add essential oils to your final rinse
If your hair is dry or greasy, add six drops of essential oil to your final rinse. If it is normal hair, you can choose your essential oil just for its effect on your hair colour.
For dark hair: Rosemary, cedarwood.
For fair hair: Camomile, lemon.

Also, adding two tablespoons of cider vinegar to the final rinse will give your hair extra shine.

Monthly conditioning treatment
Sometimes hair needs a little extra attention, in which case try this conditioning treatment.
Greasy: 50 ml almond oil, 5 ml jojoba, ten drops lemon, six drops rosemary, four drops bergamot.
Dry: 50 ml almond oil, 5 ml jojoba, ten drops sandalwood, five drops lavender, five drops camomile.
Normal: 50 ml almond oil, 5 ml jojoba, ten drops rosewood, five drops rosemary, five drops lemon.

Part your hair into sections and apply the oil liberally from the roots to the ends. Cover the hair in a warm towel and leave for half an hour (up to an hour if your hair is dry). When you come to wash the oil off, apply shampoo before you add water. Massage the shampoo well in. Then wash as usual. This way, the oil is removed more thoroughly.

For thinning hair

Use cedarwood oil in your hair products, and massage into your scalp weekly, eight to ten drops of cedarwood oil in 25 ml of oil base. Massage the scalp vigorously (perhaps ask a friend to do this for you). Cedarwood has been known to help restore hair growth.

For dandruff

Eucalyptus, rosemary and lemon essential oils will help keep dandruff at bay. Use as above in a weekly massage, and add to your usual hair products.

AROMATHERAPY AND WOMEN

The essential oils can bring relief and comfort to women during normal gynaecological conditions such as pregnancy and the menopause. They can also help relieve some of the female minor disorders, but permanent change here will only come about by serious examination of your lifestyle and diet, and the adoption of preventative tactics.

Pre-menstrual tension

Aromatherapy can give great relief to women who suffer from PMT which is a condition that affects mind and body negatively, whereas the oils affect mind and body positively. The symptoms include depression, mood swings, irritability, insomnia, water retention, lethargy, craving for sweet things, cramps and, when the period does arrive, backache. All these affect different women in different ways. Further, the symptoms may change from one month to the next, one time being physical, the next emotional.

If PMT is a real problem for you, treatment with an aromatherapist will help, but there still remains much that you can do at home. Choose a formula from below according to how the condition affects you. The oils may be used singly or in combination, using eight drops in an aromatic bath and six drops in a body rub or massage (apricot kernel or grapeseed would be a good choice for base oil as they absorb easily into the skin and feel very light).

Water retention: Juniper, fennel, cypress
Depression: Clary-sage, bergamot
Irritability: Camomile, sandalwood, lavender
Insomnia: Lavender, neroli
Mood swings: Geranium, rosewood
Lack of energy: Bergamot, grapefruit
Bloated feeling: Cypress, juniper, rosemary
Feeling unattractive: Rose, jasmine, ylang-ylang
Headache: Peppermint, lavender
Irregular/scanty periods: Myrrh, rose, cypress. There are
     also a number of oils which are said to be emmenagogues,
     i.e. they encourage menstrual flow, and will be helpful to
     women whose period is delayed or irregular. Obviously
     they should be avoided if there is any chance of pregnancy.
     The oils are: basil, clary-sage, cypress, fennel, hyssop,
     jasmine, juniper, myrrh, pennyroyal, peppermint,
     rosemary, rose, sage, thyme, wintergreen
Heavy/painful periods: Camomile, lavender, nutmeg,
     cypress.
     A hot compress is particularly comforting for a painful
     period. Make one from six to eight drops of the above oils
     in a litre of hot water and put the compress on the lower
     back and lower abdomen. Then cover in a warm towel and
     rest. If menstrual pain becomes particularly acute and is
     persistent over a long spell, consult a doctor.

Pregnancy

As well as being a very special time for a woman, pregnancy
can also be an anxious one, since the body is undergoing
unfamiliar changes as the baby develops in the womb. It is a
time when I would especially recommend regular sessions
with an aromatherapist – both during pregnancy and afterwards. Most aromatherapists are trained to deal with
pregnancy and the sessions can bring enormous relief and

comfort to a new mother, both physically and emotionally. Regular massage can prevent a build-up of tension in the lower back and neck, and can give the system a chance to rest and be pampered. It also helps the circulation and lymph system to keep functioning well.

There are certain oils which for home use are best avoided during pregnancy, especially in the first three months. The oils in question are:- clary-sage, fennel, peppermint, rosemary, cypress, cinnamon, basil, pennyroyal, hyssop, myrrh, savory, sage, thyme, origanum, jasmine, juniper, marjoram, and rose. Regular baths with camomile or lavender, however, can be very relaxing and soothing, but make sure the water is not too hot. As the months go by, you should consult your aromatherapist as to which oils she would recommend for you personally. Since pregnancy affects each woman differently, it is difficult to lay down one set formula.

Aromatherapy can also be of help in the treatment of two conditions associated with pregnancy.

Stretch marks: This is the one area where there is a set formula. Mix up a lotion from apricot kernel or peach kernel base oil and fifteen to twenty drops of essential oil. Apply this mixture throughout pregnancy to the breasts, abdomen and buttocks after a bath. Do not wait until you look big, but start from the very beginning. Some possible combinations for prevention of stretch marks are: fifteen drops tangerine or mandarin; five drops mandarin plus five drops neroli plus five drops lavender; five drops tangerine plus five lavender plus five neroli. Add any of these to 50 ml base oil.

Varicose veins: If you or a member of your family are prone to varicose veins, it is a good idea to take whatever preventative measures you can during pregnancy as this can be the start of them for some women. You should find the following helpful:

1. Sit with your feet up daily, even if it is for only ten minutes.

2. Put a pillow under the mattress at the end of your bed, so raising your feet slightly for a good long period whilst you are asleep.

3. Sit with your legs up and gently massage them with long strokes from ankle to knee to thigh, using two drops of lavender oil in 10 ml base oil.

Giving birth

At the birth itself, there are several oils that can help before and during delivery.

Fennel helps to stimulate the flow of milk and could be introduced beneficially to your massage just before the birth and afterwards.

Any oil whose scent you particularly like should be chosen to disinfect the birth room. I would recommend eucalyptus or neroli as, apart from their pleasing scents, they will help your breathing. A few drops on a radiator, light bulb or diffuser will scent the room.

The following list of oil properties may be of value in helping you decide the essential oil to fit a particular situation:

Lavender:	To relax you
Rose:	A uterine relaxant
Jasmine:	Can help with contractions
Neroli:	To calm you
Clary-sage:	Soothing and euphoric
Nutmeg:	To prime the muscles for contractions

These oils could be diluted and rubbed gently into your back during labour, or soaked in a compress and applied to your lower back and abdomen, according to which you feel would benefit you most.

After the birth

This time immediately after the birth and the weeks that follow can be most demanding, requiring a great readjustment of routine and making immense claims on your time and energy – at the very time when you need to recover from the birth. In order to help you through this period, do carry on with aromatherapy treatments if you can find the time. Otherwise, use the following oils at home:

Jasmine:	To disperse depression
Bergamot:	To uplift and revitalize
Rose:	To heal and soothe
Lavender:	For sleep and relaxation
Fennel:	To help the flow of milk
Rosemary:	To freshen and as a pick-me-up

Breast and nipple problems: If at this time, you suffer from sore or cracked nipples, try the following remedy. Mix four drops of rose and two drops of lemon in two teaspoons of almond oil, and apply to the breasts. This will help ease the soreness if applied daily, but do cleanse the area with an unperfumed cleanser before breast-feeding. To ease swollen breasts before and after the birth, put one drop of geranium in an eggcup of rosewater and apply daily. Rose, lemon and geranium oils can also be applied in a cooling compress to the breasts to ease swelling.

The menopause

Just as menstruation can affect women in totally different ways, so can the menopause. Some sail through it without any difficulty, whilst others are troubled by a variety of symptoms: hot flushes, mood swings, lack of sex drive, depression, sweating, dizziness, palpitations, fluid retention, and irregular or heavy periods.

The following oils or combinations of oils have been found

to be helpful for the various symptoms and can be used for massage or in aromatic baths.

To soothe and calm: Camomile
For balance: Geranium
For inner confidence and beauty: Jasmine
For feeling feminine and desirable: Rose
To tranquillize: Neroli, vetiver and lavender
To help sex drive: Clary-sage, jasmine and ylang-ylang
To lift depression: Bergamot, ylang-ylang and jasmine
To regulate periods: Rose and geranium
To prevent bloating: Fennel and juniper
For energy: Rosemary and bergamot
For mood swings: Camomile and sandalwood
For hot flushes: Camomile and geranium
Dizziness: Peppermint

Many women who suffer from hot flushes and dizziness also find that to cut down on stimulants such as coffee, tea and alcohol can be most helpful.

Cystitis

This can be a particularly uncomfortable and distressing complaint and, if not treated, can travel up to the kidneys where it can be extremely painful. It is an inflammation of the bladder, and the main symptoms are a burning sensation when passing water and a frequent need to do so. This can be accompanied by nausea, fever and general fatigue. Sometimes the urine is cloudy and even bloodstained. There are several steps you can take to help relieve this condition:

1. Drink as much water as possible to help flush out the infection.
2. Keep warm (a hot water bottle on the lower back is especially comforting).
3. Avoid consuming anything that can become acidic in the

system e.g. coffee, alcohol, sugar and spicy food, as this will further irritate the inflammation.

4. Drink a glass of water containing a tablespoon of bicarbonate of soda as soon as you feel an attack coming on.

5. When they are in season put a pound of cherries – stalks and all – in two pints of water and boil. Leave the mixture to steep, and drink the syrup first thing in the morning.

6. Bath in water containing essential oils. Six to eight drops of any of the following will bring some relief: bergamot, sandalwood, juniper, cajeput.

7. Mix into a base oil six drops of any of the above essential oils and apply to the lower back, abdomen and thighs. The oils are all antiseptic and will help kill any infection.

8. If the condition is very painful, a hot compress made from the above oils – six to eight drops in a pint of hot water – applied to the lower back and abdomen will bring some comfort.

If the symptoms persist, it is highly advisable to consult a doctor as the infection can be quite serious if it passes up to the kidneys. Antibiotics will probably be prescribed and, although many people these days are somewhat opposed to them, this is one time when they should not be rejected. You can carry on with your use of the essential oils during the course. As the antibiotics kill all the bacteria present – good and bad – it is a good idea to take acidophilus tablets (available at most health shops) at the same time, and for a few weeks after recovery, to replace the 'friendly' bacteria. A cheaper method of replacing the 'friendly' bacteria is to eat live yoghurt.

As a preventative measure to avoid getting cystitis in the first place, it is advisable to drink plenty of fluid regularly, and to watch your diet to ensure the intake of acidic foods is not too high.

Thrush

This is a very common complaint suffered by many women. It is caused by a yeast-like fungus called *Candida albicans* which is always present in small amounts in the vagina. Usually it is kept from growing by traces of acid produced by harmless bacteria, and so there is no irritation or symptoms. If, however, the balance in the body is upset, the fungus grows and produces from the vagina a thick, white discharge which causes irritation and itching. Some women also have a tendency to urinate more often than usual and may experience a burning or stinging sensation when doing so.

The condition can be caused by stress, general bad health or the wearing of tight jeans or underwear, and sometimes it can be brought on by the use of antibiotics. This is especially debilitating for women who take antibiotics for cystitis and end up with thrush! It can also be sexually transmitted and, as men do not suffer the symptoms as intensely as women, they may pass it on without being aware that they ever had it. To relieve and prevent thrush, take the following steps:

1. Change your diet. Cut out sugar as *Candida* thrives on it. Cake, chocolate, pastries and alcohol are all out, I am afraid. Also avoid yeast and fermented foods, e.g. vinegar, miso and soya. Some women find that fruit can irritate the condition, particularly if the fruit is slightly bruised. It is probably safest to avoid fruit during an attack of thrush, and to reintroduce it into the diet only gradually after recovery – taking care not to eat too much.

2. Wear loose-fitting clothes and if you wear nylon or polyester underwear change to cotton.

3. Avoid vaginal deodorants and chemical soaps, body shampoos and bubble baths.

4. Take acidophilus tablets (available from most health stores) or eat live yoghurt (the live bacteria in these products will help fight the *Candida*). Some women find that live

yoghurt can relieve the itching if applied on a tampon inserted into the vagina.

5. Take daily aromatic baths with six to eight drops of lavender, bergamot, myrrh or tea-tree.

6. Put two tablespoons of live yoghurt in a bowl and one drop of any of the above essential oils. Apply to a tampon and insert into the vagina. (Be careful not to overdo the essential oils, as the vaginal area is very delicate and the oils can sting if used in excess.)

7. When suffering from thrush, douche daily with the essential oils, then weekly, then monthly to prevent a recurrence. You can buy a douche at most chemists these days. Four drops of essential oil to one litre of warm water will be sufficient.

8. If the condition persists, see your doctor who may put you on a course of Nystalin. Although this will clear it, try to make the preventative measures described above part and parcel of your lifestyle to ward off frequent attacks. If you are under stress and run down, book a number of aromatherapy treatments with a practitioner to help you get back on course.

Herpes

As this is a condition that can erupt when you are under stress, anything that will prevent stress from accumulating will be extremely beneficial. The following should help:

1. If you are a victim of herpes, either ensure you have regular sessions with an aromatherapist or, if you are aware that there is a stressful time coming up, book a course of treatments for as long as it lasts.

2. Daily aromatic baths are always a good idea as the oils are both antiseptic and relaxing. Lavender for its soothing properties, and bergamot for its uplifting quality would be good choices for regular use to prevent herpes.

3. If you do have an outbreak, bathe the area in a solution

of six drops of lavender to one litre of water. Then apply eucalyptus, lavender or tea-tree on a cotton bud to the blisters. Frequent application in the beginning can prevent a bad attack.

AROMATHERAPY AND WEIGHT PROBLEMS

So many times clients have come to an aromatherapy session asking, 'Isn't there some oil that can dissolve all the fat away?' I wish there was an oil to do magic, and I wish I could make it all disappear. Sadly, there are no short cuts to healthy weight loss. Only cutting down your intake of fattening foods and taking regular exercise will bring results.

The essential oils can, however, help with the process of dieting, first by detoxification and secondly by reducing water retention. They can also help with some of the problems of weight gain, such as cellulite, stretch marks and flabbiness, and they can generally improve skin tone and appearance.

Before going further I must issue the usual warning given in these circumstances. Any strict regime or cleansing programme should be undertaken only under the supervision of a doctor or trained nutrition adviser.

Beginning a diet

I would advise anyone starting a diet programme aimed at weight loss to book themselves a weekly aromatherapy treatment. Apart from the therapeutic value, it will make you feel good just to be pampered! Even with the most well-balanced and sensible diet, you are still cutting down on food, and the body and mind are only too aware that they are being deprived. Some overweight people are so because of glandular imbalance or hereditary dispositions. Of course there are exceptions, but most of the hereditary disposition towards weight gain is simply a family trait for enjoying good food. Therefore, in order to compensate for not being able to enjoy your favourite foods, reward yourself with a fragrant, weekly massage.

DETOXIFICATION

When weight gain has come about through bad diet including items such as alcohol and excessive sugar and starch, the chances are that your system is going to be congested and a little sluggish, with a tired liver working hard to keep on top of it all. Many dieticians recommend a short cleansing period at the beginning of a diet, consisting of plenty of raw fruit, vegetables and spring water. As some of the oils are detoxifying, a regular bath or massage with juniper, fennel or rosemary would help the process of elimination to get started.

One lady, in her enthusiasm, having read that juniper oil helps in a slimming regime, poured half a bottle into her bath, thinking that the more she poured in the more effective it would be. She phoned me in desperation, having leapt out of the bath. 'My skin's on fire,' she cried, 'I'm stinging all over.' I advised her to try and wash off what she could and then to apply a base oil all over to try and dilute the concentrated oil which would have been partly absorbed by her skin. Six to eight drops, as advised throughout this book, would have been quite sufficient for her bath. Often when people embark on a diet they are in a hurry to see results and go to extremes in order to try to speed up the process. However with the oils, as with any diet programme, slow and steady wins the race.

Fluid retention

Many women suffer from this complaint, particularly just
before a period. Anther possible cause of water retention is
too much salt or too much alcohol in the diet. Incidentally, the
system can become acidic as a result of alcohol or too much
sugar. In trying to restore a balance, the body retains water
to dilute the acidity. If this is the cause, it would be wise to
look at your diet with a nutrition counsellor and get to the
root of the problem rather than to deal simply with the
symptom.

For some people it may be an allergy (dairy and wheat
allergies are quite common) which causes the retention. One
lady, after years of trying various diuretics and crash diets,
was put on a two-week diet of raw fruit and vegetables, and
told to drink 1½ litres of spring water a day. After two
weeks, she said, the bloating she had suffered for years had
gone completely.

Often women with this condition cut down on liquid
because they think they are going to retain it, when in fact
drinking plenty of water would actually help. The body would
be flushed out, and so would not need to dilute the toxicity by
retaining fluid.

The following aromatherapy oils all have diuretic properties, and for fluid retention before a period or as a part of a
detoxifying diet can be extremely useful: camomile, cedarwood, cypress, juniper, fennel, geranium, rosemary, frankincense and eucalyptus. They can be used either in an aromatic
bath or in a base oil for massage.

Lymph drainage

The main functions of the lymphatic system in the body are
the drainage and removal of fluids and the absorption of fat
from the intestines. If this system is sluggish and the
circulation is poor, not only does the body feel tired but it can
retain water generally, which causes swelling (oedema),

particularly round the ankles. It is also one of the causes of cellulite.

Many aromatherapists are trained in a particular type of massage called lymph drainage to help relieve this condition. With particular oils chosen to stimulate the system into functioning properly, they will follow the lines of the lymph system in the body in a smooth, vigorous massage (from the hands to the armpits, from the ankle to the groin, up to the collarbone). The oils used for this are:

Fennel:	Cleansing and diuretic
Juniper:	Detoxifying, diuretic and good for a sluggish liver
Black pepper:	Stimulating
Rosemary:	Stimulating and cleansing
Geranium:	Helps to restore balance and also used as a diuretic
Cypress:	Sometimes used for its positive effect on circulation

Most aromatherapists will also recommend vigorous daily skin brushing to keep the lymph flowing. Follow the lines of the lymph drainage massage (i.e. from hands up to the collarbone, and ankles up to the groin, then to the collarbone.) Use long, sweeping strokes using a skin brush which can be purchased at health shops or stores such as Body Shop.

Stretch marks

Sadly, stretch marks cannot be eliminated once they are there, although they do fade slightly with time. The general tone and texture of the skin can, however, be improved immensely with aromatherapy.

Measures can be taken to prevent these stretch marks. If you have put on weight and want to lose it and you do not wish to find that your skin, having been stretched, is marked, use the essential oils. Even when at your largest, regular body rubs and massage will help. Look after the skin before losing weight or dieting, and you can prevent the marks. This is preferable to waiting until you are thin, your skin has shrunk, and it is too late. The best oils to deal with stretch marks are mandarin, tangerine and neroli. See p. 124 for combination recipes.

Cellulite

The bane of many women's lives, cellulite is the name given to the pockets of fat that deposit themselves usually around the thighs, hips and buttocks, and occasionally on the stomach and upper arms. It looks like spongy orange peel when squeezed – bumpy and uneven. Amongst the causes are hormonal changes, bad circulation, junk and refined foods, sugar, alcohol, smoking, stress and lack of exercise. Aromatherapy can help this condition but, as with many disorders that reveal themselves on the surface of the body, change has to come from within.

I had one client who was determined to get to grips with her cellulite. She embarked on a particularly fierce exercise programme and had regular aromatherapy sessions for cellulite, as well as daily skin brushing at home. She stopped smoking, and when we discussed her diet she insisted it comprised mainly wholefoods, fresh fruit and vegetables. So I could not understand why, after five weeks, the improvement was minimal. She seemed to be taking all the right steps. Finally she sheepishly admitted to eating two packets of Rowntree's fruit pastilles every day – a habit begun fifteen years previously and continued ever since. 'It's only a little candy,' she said. 'I didn't think it would make any difference!' Often the substance that we enjoy most and have the most difficulty giving up is the one that is causing the problem. With great self-control the lady gave up her sweets, after which the improvement in her legs was really obvious. She now looks marvellous.

Here are some steps you can take to combat cellulite.

1. Take regular exercise.
2. Start skin brushing (as for lymphatic drainage).
3. Avoid alcohol, tea and coffee.
4. No sweets, chocolates, pastries, salty or smoked food (these cause the body to retain more water).
5. Eat plenty of raw fruit and vegetables.
6. Drink plenty of spring water.
7. Take aromatic baths using six to eight drops of juniper, fennel, cypress or rosemary. (After or during the bath, massage and pummel the cellulite areas with a massage glove or loofah.)
8. Book regular sessions with an aromatherapist who will treat your cellulite; alternatively if you cannot afford them, make up your own blend and apply it daily. Using a base oil of grapeseed or almond oil, add a mixture of three of the following essential oils: black pepper, cypress, juniper, rosemary, fennel, geranium and lemon. Use ten drops of essential oil to 20 ml of base oil.
9. Once a week, make a hot compress from the above oils and hot water (ten drops in a bowl of water). Apply to the area and then wrap it in warm towels. This will help the penetration of the oils and intensify the detoxifying process.

Cellulite does not arrive overnight and it is certainly not going to disappear overnight. But if you follow these steps you will see a noticeable difference in a month, and if you persist it is actually possible to eliminate it completely. If you have a tendency to cellulite, you have to be consistent with your prevention tactics as it can easily recur.

Eating through depression or stress

Some people turn to food or drink at stressful times or low periods in their lives. In this case, it would be advisable to

alternate the cleansing aromatherapy treatments, which will
help the body, with a more relaxing treatment for the mind
and psyche to help relieve some of the stress which may well
be causing the overeating in the first place. It can be a vicious
circle:

Stress

Low energy
and depression   Overeating

Weight gain

Using essential oils that relax the nervous system and
promote a feeling of wellbeing and new vitality can help break
the cycle and produce instead a positive *forward* progression:

Stress → Aromatic massage → Feeling of wellbeing → New
determination and vitality.

The oils I would recommend if you are feeling large,
unattractive and unappealing are:

Bergamot: Fresh and uplifting; excellent for expelling the
              'clouds'
Jasmine: Can give a sense of inner beauty
Rose: With its delicate fragrance, it evokes a sense of
              the feminine (as opposed to being heavy and
              weighed down)
Ylang-ylang: Another feminine fragrance which relaxes and
              uplifts, leaving a light mellow feeling
Rosewood: Has an uplifting effect on the emotional state
              while being very calming (a typical effect of the
              'woods')
Geranium: For balance (often overweight people can
              become somewhat fraught and want to do
              something extreme. Geranium will help restore

a more sensible approach with its ability to bring mind and body back into balance.)

Use any one or a combination of three in an aromatic bath or massage oil, so that at least you feel good and positive enough to get on with the task of *looking* good!

THE SENSUAL SIDE OF AROMATHERAPY

Just recently at a friend's wedding, a wife of some years was heard to comment how, in the old days, the young bride was nervous not only because of the wedding itself but also because it would be her first time in the 'marriage bed'. How things have changed! In these days of sex before marriage the bride has a different fear – that there may be no sex *after* marriage, having been assured by all her married friends that it can become virtually non-existent. That may be a cynical comment, but it is sadly true for many people, since what starts out as a potent and spontaneous attraction can fade to an agreed compromise of 'Now and then, if I'm in the mood.'

In the days of ancient Rome, rose petals were strewn on the marriage bed to keep away anxiety. But what of today? With the divorce rate so high, what can we do to give confidence and stave off anxiety about a diminishing sex life, one of the prime causes of the break-up of so many marriages?

As in all areas of aromatherapy, such a subject has to be looked at holistically. Although some of the oils are known aphrodisiacs, it is not as simple as 'two drops of this and two drops of that' to make everything well. They can, however, help in certain areas that affect us sexually.

At the beginning of a love affair, the discovery of a new being is aphrodisiac enough. It is all new and exciting and arousal comes easily, with the joy of discovering each other's pleasure. As time goes by, though, different factors can enter people's lives and come between partners, causing lack of desire without its being intended. Sometimes this is not even realized until it has become a problem. This is where aromatherapy can assist. I am sure that, whatever method you choose to employ in using essential oils, you will find them an invaluable aid to your sensual life.

Stress

For many people, sexual arousal can diminish if they are worried about work, money or relationships. Sometimes sex is used to relieve this stress as a means of escape, and sometimes it is not sought at all until the period of anxiety is over. This can unfortunately leave a partner feeling neglected or bemused. What better than to deal with the stress directly? In other words alleviate the tension (which can block so many deeper feelings) with a good massage to soothe it all away. It is very difficult to feel 'sexy' if your mind is preoccupied with worry. Since it is important to be relaxed before sex, an aromatic massage will help to do this. Any of the oils for relaxation will do: neroli, lavender, ylang-ylang, sandalwood or rosewood. (See also Chapter 3.)

Lack of confidence

A negative self-image about either your body or performance can stop people becoming aroused. Jasmine is an excellent oil for giving confidence and an inner sense of beauty. Rose can enhance an air of the 'feminine' with its light, sensual fragrance. The oils can be used either in a bath or for massage. A non-sexual massage can be an encouraging way to start overcoming fear of performance, especially for many men who feel they have got to be 'good in bed' as part of their macho image. It can bring about a relaxation and feeling of ease at being touched and also an enjoyment of the sensation without feeling that something has to be given back. For some people, it is the only time they are ever touched without feeling they have got to 'perform'. If, however, the problem is deeply rooted, some sessions with a counsellor would be strongly advisable as this gives an opportunity to talk it through and discover the real cause of the problem.

Good health

Again, it is very hard to feel sexy if you are run down and not well. In fact, most people find that their libido is affected by bad health and only returns when they are back to normal. Good diet and a balanced lifestyle are indispensable for wellbeing and a healthy sex life.

Exercise

Lack of exercise can result in an unfit body, sluggishness and a lack of sexual response. Starting an exercise programme combined with some aromatherapy treatments, using stimulating and revitalizing oils, will put you in touch with the physical side of your nature again. Most people find that they not only look and feel better but also feel more sexual. Good oils for revitalizing (bath or massage) are rosemary, ginger, bergamot and basil.

Communication

During sex, we are at our most vulnerable and intimate with our partner. It is an area where sadly all sorts of unspoken grievances and resentments can come to the fore, having been pushed aside during the day. Sex can sometimes be used as a weapon to wound or reject. For example, how many times does one partner hurt the other, perhaps by some unconscious action or statement? Then the next time the wounding partner wants sex, the other, feeling aggrieved, is conveniently 'not in the mood'. Thus the errant partner is left feeling rejected, sometimes without being really aware that he or she had upset the partner in the first place. A pattern can become established. The rejected one now awaits his/her turn to even up the score by giving the cold shoulder. It sounds so petty, but it does happen.

Daily miscommunications and misunderstandings work themselves out on a sexual battlefield, leaving couples wondering, months later, what happened. What went wrong? Lack of communication – the biggest factor in partnership break-ups. Again, seeing a cousellor is often the best course of action. Partners can learn how to talk to each other again and express what is felt as it arises – rather than bottling the resentment up so much that it causes sexual blocks.

A gentle aromatic massage can also assist here, as sometimes when the right words cannot be found the physical touch can be a start. Through gentle, non-verbal contact communication is at least reopened, and with the right oils resentment can be eased and the beginning of trust re-established. Choose any combination of one to three oils from the list below and mix in a vegetable base oil in the usual way before applying to the skin.

Melissa:	Has a beneficial effect on deep anxiety
Rose:	Heals
Geranium:	Creates a feeling of harmony
Bergamot:	Lifts depression
Neroli:	Helps calm a 'charged' emotional state
Sandalwood:	Relaxes, and chases away bitterness

The roles we play

The different roles we play in life sometimes get in the way of our feeling sexual. So many women complain that all day they are 'mummy' – wiping babies' bottoms, cooking, clearing up and so on – with the result that it is hard to have to switch gear suddenly and feel sensual or even remotely sexy. And it is not necessarily any easier for men and women who work outside the home – coming home from a hard day at the office, driving through rush-hour traffic, just longing to get home, put their feet up and switch off. But what if their partner wants them to switch on? How do they bridge the gap? This is an area where the essential oils could really help, because they can affect and change moods and provide a sensuous bridge from one mood to another.

Using the oils to bridge the gap

The essential oils can be used in several ways to evoke a sensual mood.

Aromatic baths: After a long day, linger in a scented bath (with six to eight drops of the oils listed below). It will definitely undo the tensions of the day and mellow your mood.

Massage: Again, use a selection from the list below. Before actually starting the massage (e.g. while your partner is having his/her aromatic bath) read and follow the tips for creating atmosphere on p. 94. Choose an oil (or oils) from the selection given below to add to your base oil. The following are renowned for their aphrodisiac properties: rose, jasmine, ylang-ylang, patchouli, sandalwood and clary-sage. These could be used with the following, which are stimulating and warming: cardamom, black pepper, ginger cinnamon, nutmeg, coriander and cumin. Frankincense could be added for its ability to open the heart and aid communication; also benzoin for its power to induce warm, lazy feelings. Here are some formulas you might like to try:

Exotic:	Ylang-ylang and sandalwood
Stimulating:	Ylang-ylang, ginger and black pepper
Euphoric:	Clary-sage, patchouli and jasmine
Luxurious:	Rose, sandalwood and ylang-ylang
If depressed:	Rose, benzoin and ylang-ylang

If tired:	Rose, sandalwood and neroli
If anxious:	Rose, sandalwood and neroli
If uninterested:	Clary-sage and sandalwood
Feeling flat:	Ylang-ylang and black pepper (combines to smell of carnations)

As mentioned in Chapter 3, I believe the best way to learn to do massage is by seeing it done and experiencing it by having a massage yourself. Where better to apply such a skill than in your own private life? It is definitely worth the trouble of a few evening classes or a weekend course in order to learn basic techniques and strokes. From there you can experiment in whichever way you and your partner choose. Compared to the money and time people spend on perfume, cosmetics and new outfits, in the hope of making themselves attractive and keeping love alive, learning the skills of basic massage is easily a better investment for you to make since the outcome will be far more effective. The potency of touch is far-reaching in terms of pleasure as well as healing. It also gives partners a chance to discover each other's whole body and the sensual potential all over, as opposed to just the 'sexual' areas which tend to get all the attention when couples do not give each other time to explore. (NB Do not massage the genitals directly with essential oils, as they may sting on such a sensitive area.)

Scenting the room: Because the power of smell and the essential oils work directly on the limbic region of our brain (which also governs much to do with our sexuality and emotions), scent can evoke arousal and unlock many deeper hidden feelings. (Think of the consistent association of perfume with romance which is used in advertising, and of the way a scent can evoke the memory of a person or moment more vividly than any other stimulus.) By burning essential oils in a room, you can create the atmosphere you choose. In previous chapters I have spoken of burning oils for more medicinal purposes, such as to kill viruses and prevent bacteria spreading. In the present context it is for the sheer joy and atmosphere of an appealing fragrance. There are several methods of doing this.

1. Place a few drops on a candle wick before lighting.
2. Place a few drops on a light bulb.
3. Put six to eight drops in a bowl of warm water placed under a radiator.
4. If you have an open fire, put a few drops on the wood or coal.
5. Put a few drops on a diffuser (a pot made specially for burning oil.) Place a nightlight under the pot and the fragrance will fill the room.
6. Add some oil to a water spray and simply spray the air.

See following table for a guide to creating various sensual atmospheres:

Cosy:	Patchouli
Reassuring:	Rosewood
Exotic:	Ylang-ylang and sandalwood
Spicy and warm:	Cinnamon, orange and ginger (or clove)
Lazy and warm:	Benzoin
Festive:	Frankincense and myrrh

Of course, after some experimenting you could choose your own according to personal taste, and you will no doubt discover favourites as you go along.

You can also scent bedlinen by adding a few drops of your favourite oil to the water in a steam iron before ironing bedlinen, or add it to the water spray. But don't put the oils directly on to fabric or they will stain it.

As some of the oils can leave a faint trace of scent and oil on clothing (although most does get absorbed into the skin) it is advisable to use old towels and to wear older clothes after aromatherapy, especially if having regular sessions. (Incidentally for towels and clothes with oil traces, sometimes washing powder isn't enough to remove it completely, using dishwasher powder however does do the trick.)

8

A–Z OF OILS AND THEIR PROPERTIES

There are approximately three hundred essential oils in the world today, but many of them you will never come across and so I have indexed only those in common use. As you will see, most of the oils have many different properties. In order to help you choose which oil you want at any given moment, the properties and uses for which each oil is most often used are given in *italics*. You will find some oils such as lavender have many properties in italics, and others very few. This is because, although other oils may have similar properties, they are more scarce or their scent is not as popular.

Oil: Angelica
Part of plant from which oil is obtained: Seeds, roots
Properties and uses: Coughs, fevers, colds, flu, nervous exhaustion, digestion, flatulence, grounding (bringing down to earth)

Oil: Aniseed
Part of plant from which oil is obtained: Seed pod
Properties and uses: Bronchitis, catarrh, coughs, heart tonic, stimulates the circulation

Oil: Basil
Part of plant from which oil is obtained: Whole plant
Properties and uses: Nerve tonic, improves the memory.
Bronchitis, *respiratory complaints,* colds, gout, *loss of concentration,* migraine, *mental fatigue,* warts, snakebite, difficult periods, epilepsy, *fainting,* insomnia, *asthma*

Oil: Bay
Part of plant from which oil is obtained: Leaves
Properties and uses: Warms and strengthens, pulmonary antiseptic, tonic. *Colds, flu, bronchitis, sinusitis,* pneumonia, *rheumatism*

Oil: Benzoin
Part of plant from which oil is obtained: Trunk
Properties and uses: Digestive, *gentle sedative. Respiratory complaints,* asthma, skin problems, *chapped hands,* melanosis, arthritis

Oil: Bergamot
Part of plant from which oil is obtained: Peel of fruit
Properties and uses: Uplifting in depression and for general fatigue, restores appetite, tonic. Intestinal problems, digestion, wounds, scars, *acne, herpes,* eczema, psoriasis, varicose ulcers, *cystitis,* bad breath. (Take care not to use if going in the sun)

Oil: Cedarwood
Part of plant from which oil is obtained: Wood
Properties and uses: Diuretic, helps encourage sexual response. *Hair loss,* respiratory problems, sprains, *fractures,* acne, arthritis, urinary disorders, cystitis, eczema, lymphatic circulation

Oil: Cinnamon
Part of plant from which oil is obtained: Twigs, leaves
Properties and uses: Appetite stimulant, thermo-regulator, *warming in winter,* respiratory stimulant. *Convalescence,* flu, *rheumatism, sluggish digestion,* frigidity, toothache, wasp stings, snakebite, circulation, heart

Oil: Clary-sage
Part of plant from which oil is obtained: Flowering tops
Properties and uses: Euphoric, muscle relaxant, *diuretic,* tonic. Boils, *frigidity, impotence,* sore throat, skin care, *depression, menstrual cramps,* asthma

Oil: Clove
Part of plant from which oil is obtained: Flower buds
Properties and uses: Nausea, bronchitis, flatulence, *toothache, infections,* arthritis, difficult digestion, sores, general weakness

Oil: Coriander
Part of plant from which oil is obtained: Seed of fruit, leaves
Properties and uses: Indigestion, flu, fatigue, rheumatism, *loss of appetite,* constipation, *flatulence*

Oil: Cumin
Part of plant from which oil is obtained: Seeds, fruit
Properties and uses: Indigestion, headache, liver problems

Oil: Cypress
Part of plant from which oil is obtained: Leaves, twigs
Properties and uses: Diuretic. Rheumatism, *circulation, varicose veins, thread veins,* haemorrhoids, *coughs, irregular menstrual cycle,* asthma, flu, liver disorders, *cellulite, sweaty feet,* irritability, wounds

Oil: Eucalyptus
Part of plant from which oil is obtained: Leaves, twigs
Properties and uses: Respiratory complaints, coughs, colds, sinusitis, cystitis, rheumatics, cuts, burns, fever, fungal infections, *sore throats,* migraine, herpes, mosquito repellent, strained muscles

Oil: Fennel
Part of plant from which oil is obtained: Seeds
Properties and uses: Digestive, diuretic. Nausea, constipation, menopausal problems, post-natal (congestion of the breasts – it helps the flow of milk), flatulence, *helps regulate the menstrual cycle,* kidney stones, chest problems

Oil: Frankincense
Part of plant from which oil is obtained: Bark
Properties and uses: Respiratory problems (bronchitis, coughs), laryngitis, *skin care (ageing skin, wrinkles,* ulcers, wounds, nerve tonic, stimulates brain, slows down breathing, *cleanser spiritually* and physically (often burnt in churches)

Oil: Galbanum
Part of plant from which oil is obtained: Bark
Properties and uses: Encourages scar tissue to heal, respiratory problems, swellings, nervous conditions

Oil: Garlic
Properties and uses: Detoxifier, decongestant. *Rheumatism, flu,* asthma, *colds,* coughs, intestinal parasites, warts, wounds, insect bites, ulcers

Oil: Geranium
Part of plant from which oil is obtained: Leaves, stalks,
  flowers
Properties and uses: Tonic, *balancer,* diuretic, skin toner.
  Circulation, *mastitis, bad skin conditions* (sores, acne),
  wounds, burns, dry eczema, chilblains, frostbite,
  depression, mosquito repellent

Oil: Ginger
Part of plant from which oil is obtained: Roots
*Properties and uses: Digestive, warming. Rheumatism,
  muscular aches and pains, colds,* sprains, nausea,
  diarrhoea, appetite loss, flatulence

Oil: Grapefruit
Part of plant from which oil is obtained: Rind of fruit
Properties and uses: Tonic, digestive, *freshener.* Liver and
  kidney problems

Oil: Hyssop
Part of plant from which oil is obtained: Leaves, flowering
  tops
Properties and uses: Bruises, rheumatism, arthritis, coughs,
  colds, viral infections, asthma, hay fever, eczema,
  circulatory problems

Oil: Jasmine (known as king of the oils)
Part of plant from which oil is obtained: Flowers
Properties and uses: Calming, aphrodisiac (can give a sense
  of internal beauty). *Depression, menstrual cramps,
  excessive release of emotion, skin care (dry skin), labour
  pains* (can strengthen contractions), anxiety, post-natal
  depression

Oil: Juniper
Part of plant from which oil is obtained: Berries
Properties and uses: Diuretic, digestive, appetite stimulant.
  Liver, hangovers, rheumatism, *cellulite,* coughs, acne,
  urinary disorders, cystitis, period pains, eczema,
  psoriasis, ulcers, wounds, flatulence, *clogged system,*
  detoxifying for mind and body

Oil: Lavender
Part of plant from which oil is obtained: Flowering tops
Properties and uses: Digestive. Irritability, stress, pain,
  rheumatics, fainting, pulmonary conditions, *urinary*
  disorders, coughs, colds, cystitis, migraine, sunstroke,
  sunburn, skin problems (acne, eczema, psoriasis),
  snakebite, insect stings, burns, high blood pressure,
  headaches, insomnia, muscle spasm, stomach upsets

Oil: Lemon
Part of plant from which oil is obtained: Rind of fruit
Properties and uses: Tonic, astringent, diuretic. Lowers
  blood pressure, purifies liver, insect repellent, restores
  appetite, ageing skin, arthritis, colds, flu, skin blemishes,
  blood and breath purifier, cellulite, arthritis

Oil: Lemon grass
Part of plant from which oil is obtained: Whole plant
Properties and uses: Tonic. Slow digestion, blocked intestines,
  migraine, headaches, respiratory problems, insufficient
  milk after childbirth, panic attacks

Oil: Lime
Part of plant from which oil is obtained: Rind of fruit
Properties and uses: Astringent, tonic, freshener. Headaches,
  rheumatism

Oil: Mandarin
Part of plant from which oil is obtained: Rind of fruit
Properties and uses: Digestive, soothing tonic. Prevention of stretch marks, liver problems, *anxiety,* oily skin

Oil: Marjoram
Part of plant from which oil is obtained: Flowering tops, leaves
Properties and uses: Insomnia, migraine, nervous stomach, sprains, bruises, colds, rheumatism, *menstrual problems,* asthma, bronchitis, arthritis, flatulence, constipation, colds

Oil: Melissa
Part of plant from which oil is obtained: Leaves
Properties and uses: Sedative, digestive. Heart tonic, palpitations, *deep anxiety, allergies, nervousness,* migraine, shock, *menstrual problems, asthma, mellows the mood* and chases away black thoughts (particularly good for bitter people)

Oil: Myrrh
Part of plant from which oil is obtained: Bark, resin
Properties and uses: Skin care, helps menstrual flow, bronchitis, *laryngitis,* catarrh, coughs, *urinary disorders, infections, flatulence,* dispels dark moods, *fungal infections (Candida),* mouth and skin ulcers

Oil: Myrtle
Part of plant from which oil is obtained: Young leaves
Properties and uses: Touchiness, asthma, skin, digestion, *respiratory problems*

Oil: Neroli
Part of plant from which oil is obtained: Flowers
Properties and uses: Calming (almost hypnotically so),
   digestive. Acne, eczema, *skin care,* insomnia, nervous
   system, *cardiac,* lowers high blood pressure, *anxiety,*
   menopausal problems, depression, shock, dermatitis

Oil: Niaouli
Part of plant from which oil is obtained: Leaves, twigs
*Properties and uses: Respiratory problems, colds, flu,
   sinusitis, sore throats,* cystitis, wounds, sores, burns,
   strengthens the immune system, purifies the atmosphere,
   diarrhoea

Oil: Nutmeg
Part of plant from which oil is obtained: Seed
Properties and uses: Nausea, vomiting, muscular aches and
   pains, rheumatism, arthritis, acne, respiratory problems,
   bad breath, diarrhoea

Oil: Olibanum
Part of plant from which oil is obtained: Resin
Properties and uses: Uplifting, helps concentration. Mastitis,
   asthma, bronchitis, ulcers, wounds, air purifier

Oil: Orange
Part of plant from which oil is obtained: Rind of fruit
Properties and uses: Tonic, *constipation,* travel sickness,
   stomach, mouth problems (gum disease and ulcers),
   depression, tranquillizer

Oil: Origanum (oregano)
Part of plant from which oil is obtained: Leaves, flowering
   tops
Properties and uses: Digestive. *Bronchitis,* respiratory
   problems, *viral infections,* rheumatism, loss of appetite

Oil: Parsley
Part of plant from which oil is obtained: Seeds
Properties and uses: Tonic, *diuretic*. Kidney problems

Oil: Patchouli
Part of plant from which oil is obtained: Leaves
Properties and uses: Diuretic. Skin inflammation, insect
   repellent, broken skin (helps cells regenerate), scars,
   acne, *eczema*, burns, herpes, *tired skin*, anxiety,
   encourages sexual response, *relaxing*

Oil: Peppermint
Part of plant from which oil is obtained: Whole plant
*Properties and uses: Stimulant. Nausea, travel sickness,
   vomiting, indigestion,* flatulence, *migraine, headaches,
   liver problems,* arthritis, *blood cleanser,* skin complaints,
   eczema, acne, bruises, ulcers, painful periods, mosquito
   repellent, *flu, colds, sinusitis,* palpitations, *bad breath,
   sweaty feet*

Oil: Petitgrain
Part of plant from which oil is obtained: Leaves, twigs
Properties and uses: Insomnia, depression, *convalescence,*
   strengthens nervous system

Oil: Pine
Part of plant from which oil is obtained: Needles, twigs
Properties and uses: Diuretic, tonic. *Respiratory problems,
   colds, flu, sinusitis, bronchitis, cystitis,* rheumatism,
   bladder and kidney problems, sore throat, muscular aches
   and pains, water retention, air purifier, *period pains*

Oil: Rose (known as queen of the oils)
Part of plant from which oil is obtained: Petals
Properties and uses: Aphrodisiac, healer. PMT, menopause, *skin care, depression,* acne, eczema, thread veins, *deep grief and numbness, shock, psychic disorders,* dreaminess, heart tonic (emotionally, physically and psychologically), post-natal, *dry skin,* puffiness, constipation, *frigidity*

Oil: Rosemary
Part of plant from which oil is obtained: Flowers, leaves
Properties and uses: Tonic, diuretic. Asthma, *respiratory,* heart stimulant, rheumatism, burns, *regulates painful periods, sprains, swollen ankles, headaches, gout, muscular aches and pains, (sports strains), liver, decongestant, bronchitis, hair tonic, hair loss, fainting, fatigue,* flatulence, *general stimulant*

Oil: Rosewood
Part of plant from which oil is obtained: Wood
Properties and uses: Uplifting, cheering, steadying on nerves. Skin allergies, headaches, *depression*

Oil: Sage
Part of plant from which oil is obtained: Leaves, flowers
Properties and uses: Diuretic, stimulant, blood purifier, tonic. Thrush, eczema, sprains, bronchitis, sweating, asthma, strained muscles, sluggish digestion, insect bites and stings, preparation for childbirth

Oil: Sandalwood
Part of plant from which oil is obtained: Wood
Properties and uses: Calming, aphrodisiac. Cystitis, urinary disorders, sore throat, dry skin, eczema, sores, puffy face

Oil: Spearmint
Part of plant from which oil is obtained: Leaves, flowering
   tops
Properties and uses: Digestive, nausea, fevers, bad breath

Oil: Tangerine
Part of plant from which oil is obtained: Rind of fruit
Properties and uses: Rheumatism, cellulite, *stretch marks,*
   nerve tonic, *stomach*

Oil: Tea-tree
Part of plant from which oil is obtained: Leaves, twigs
*Properties and uses: Fungal infections, viral and bacterial
   infections, colds, flu, warts, cold sores,* acne, shock,
   verrucae, snakebite, *thrush,* insect repellent, *athlete's foot*

Oil: Thuja
Part of plant from which oil is obtained: Leaves, bark
Properties and uses: Cystitis, verrucae, warts

Oil: Thyme
Part of plant from which oil is obtained: Leaves, flowering
   tops
Properties and uses: Stimulant, diuretic, tonic. Rheumatism,
   aches, pains, circulation, hair loss, warts, wounds, burns,
   urinary disorders, asthma, coughs, intestinal infections,
   stings, fatigue, gum and teeth care, regulates scanty
   periods

Oil: Vetiver (known as the oil of tranquility)
Part of plant from which oil is obtained: Roots
Properties and uses: Calming. Insomnia, rheumatism, liver
   decongestant, balances the *nervous system, anxiety*

Oil: Violet leaves
Part of plant from which oil is obtained: Leaves
Properties and uses: Diuretic. Respiratory, fibrositis,
   rheumatism, liver decongestant

Oil: Ylang-ylang
Part of plant from which oil is obtained: Flowers
Properties and uses: Aphrodisiac, relaxes and uplifts. Hyper-
   ventilating, *hair and skin care, balance,* respiratory
   problems, *regulates and calms the heart,* palpitations,
   insect bites, *irritability, high blood pressure*

MAJOR PROPERTIES AND ASSOCIATED OILS

Analgesic: Bergamot, camomile, camphor, eucalyptus, geranium, lavender, marjoram, peppermint, rosemary.

Antibiotic: Bergamot, camomile, cinnamon, clove, eucalyptus, garlic, hyssop, juniper, lavender, lemon, lime, myrtle, niaouli, onion, origanum, patchouli, pine, tea-tree, thyme.

Anti-fungal: Eucalyptus, juniper, lavender, lemon, myrtle, patchouli, sage, sandalwood, tea-tree, thyme.

Antiseptic: All of them are antiseptic but particularly good are bergamot, eucalyptus, juniper.

Anti-viral: Bergamot, cinnamon, clove, eucalyptus, garlic, lavender, onion, parsley, sandalwood, tea-tree, thyme.

Aphrodisiac: Black pepper, clary-sage, ginger, jasmine, neroli, patchouli, rose, sandalwood, ylang-ylang.

Diuretic: Benzoin, black pepper, camomile, cedarwood, cypress, eucalyptus, fennel, frankincense, geranium, hyssop, juniper, lavender, rosemary, sandalwood.

Expectorant: Basil, benzoin, bergamot, cedarwood, eucalyptus, fennel, hyssop, marjoram, myrrh, peppermint, sandalwood.

Laxative: Black pepper, camphor, fennel, marjoram, rose.

Sedative: Benzoin, bergamot, camomile, camphor, cedarwood, clary-sage, cypress, geranium, jasmine, juniper, lavender, marjoram, melissa, myrrh, neroli, patchouli, rose, sandalwood, ylang-ylang.

Skin tonic: Bergamot, camphor, cypress, geranium, juniper, lemon, rosemary.

Stimulant: Black pepper, camphor, eucalyptus, peppermint, rosemary.

Tonic: Basil, black pepper, camomile, cardamom, clary-sage, fennel, frankincense, geranium, grapefruit, jasmine, juniper, lavender, marjoram, melissa, myrrh, neroli, patchouli, rose, sandalwood.

A–Z OF MINOR DISORDERS AND APPROPRIATE OILS

This index is a quick reference guide to which oils you can use for different conditions. For some conditions the choice is quite wide. In such instances the oils I would choose are in italics. You may find as you become more familiar with the oils that you prefer others – all of them are therapeutic, italicized or not. Mouthwashes and gargles should be diluted in the ratio of two drops of oil to half a pint of water.

Condition or requirement: Abscesses
Oil: Lavender, bergamot, camomile
Method of application: Compress

Condition or requirement: Acne
Oil: Patchouli, tea-tree, *bergamot, lemon, juniper,* sandalwood, geranium
Method of application: Compress, skin preparation

Condition or requirement: Ageing skin
Oil: Frankincense, patchouli, lavender, *rose,* geranium, carrot, *lemon*
Method of application: Skin preparation

Condition or requirement: Allergies
Oil: Camomile, melissa, lavender
Method of application: Compress, bath

Condition or requirement: Anxiety
Oil: Neroli, lavender, vetiver, rosewood, bergamot,
   sandalwood, patchouli, ylang-ylang, mandarin
Method of application: Massage, bath

Condition or requirement: Aphrodisiac
Oil: Ylang-ylang, sandalwood, rose, jasmine, clary-sage
Method of application: Bath, massage

Condition or requirement: Appetite (loss of)
Oil: Cinnamon, fennel, camomile, cardamom, bergamot,
   origanum
Method of application: Bath, massage

Condition or requirement: Arthritis
Oil: Rosemary, eucalyptus, juniper, ginger, cypress, cajeput,
   benzoin
Method of application: Compress, bath, massage

Condition or requirement: Asthma
Oil: Benzoin, cypress, eucalyptus, marjoram, melissa, basil,
   myrtle
Method of application: Massage, inhalation

Condition or requirement: Athlete's foot
Oil: Tea-tree, myrtle
Method of application: Compress

Condition or requirement: Bad breath (see Halitosis)

Condition or requirement: Baldness
Oil: Rosemary, cedarwood
Method of application: Massage, hair preparations

Condition or requirement: Boils
Oil: Camomile, lavender, bergamot, juniper, clary-sage
Method of application: Compress

Condition or requirement: Breasts (see Mastitis)

Condition or requirement: Bronchitis
Oil: Basil, *benzoin,* frankincense, lavender, peppermint, rosemary, *camphor,* sandalwood, *pine,* bay, *cajeput,* origanum
Method of application: Inhalation, massage

Condition or requirement: Bruises
Oil: Lavender, camphor, hyssop
Method of application: Compress

Condition or requirement: Burns
Oil: Lavender, camomile, eucalyptus, geranium
Method of application: Compress

Condition or requirement: Candida (see Thrush)

Condition or requirement: Capillaries (see Thread veins)

Condition or requirement: Catarrh
Oil: Cajeput, eucalyptus, niaouli, pine
Method of application: Inhalation

Condition or requirement: Cellulite
Oil: Juniper, black pepper, clary-sage, *cypress,* geranium, *rosemary,* tangerine
Method of application: Massage, bath, compress

Condition or requirement: Chapped skin
Oil: Benzoin, camomile, lavender
Method of application: Compress, massage

Condition or requirement: Chicken pox
Oil: Camomile, lavender, eucalytpus, bergamot, tea-tree
Method of application: Compress, bath

Condition or requirement: Chilblains
Oil: Cypress, black pepper, marjoram, rosemary, juniper
Method of application: Massage, bath

Condition or requirement: Childbirth
Oil: Jasmine, lavender
Method of application: Massage, bath

Condition or requirement: Circulation (poor)
Oil: Lavender, *cypress*, clary-sage, ylang-ylang, rosemary,
    cedarwood, geranium
Method of application: Massage, bath

Condition or requirement: Colds
Oil: Basil, camphor, bay, *niaouli*, *peppermint*, *eucalyptus*,
    tea-tree, *rosemary*, garlic, hyssop
Method of application: Inhalation, bath

Condition or requirement: Cold sores (see Herpes)

Condition or requirement: Conjunctivitis
Oil: Camomile, rose, lavender
Method of application: Compress (never put oil directly on
    eyes or eye area)

Condition or requirement: Constipation
Oil: Black pepper, bergamot, *fennel*, rose, juniper, lemon
    grass, rosemary, *coriander*, orange
Method of application: Massage

Condition or requirement: Convalescence
Oil: Cinnamon, bergamot, ginger, petitgrain
Method of application: Bath, massage

Condition or requirement: Coughs
Oil: Benzoin, frankincense, *eucalyptus*, myrrh, rosemary,
    cypress, peppermint, pine
Method of application: Inhalation, bath

Condition or requirement: Cystitis
Oil: Bergamot, rose, *lavender*, juniper, *sandalwood*,
    cedarwood, pine
Method of application: Massage, bath, douche

Condition or requirement: Deodorant
Oil: Peppermint, bergamot, rosemary, neroli, lime, lavender
Method of application: Bath

Condition or requirement: Depression
Oil: Basil, *bergamot, clary-sage, jasmine,* geranium,
    rosewood, neroli, rose, sandalwood, *ylang-ylang,* melissa
Method of application: Bath, massage

Condition or requirement: Dermatitis
Oil: Benzoin, camomile, geranium, juniper, *lavender,* neroli,
    nutmeg
Method of application: Massage, compress

Condition or requirement: Diarrhoea
Oil: Black pepper, camomile, camphor, cypress, niaouli,
    peppermint, rosemary, sandalwood, fennel, benzoin
Method of application: Massage, bath, compress

Condition or requirement: Digestion (see Stomach)

Condition or requirement: Disinfectant
Oil: Bergamot, *eucalyptus,* juniper, lavender
Method of application: Vaporizer, air spray

Condition or requirement: Diuretic
Oil: Fennel, juniper, clary-sage, cypress, eucalyptus
Method of application: Massage, bath

Condition or requirement: Dry skin
Oil: Sandalwood, rose, lavender, geranium
Method of application: Skin preparation

Condition or requirement: Dysentery
Oil: Black pepper, camomile, cypress
Method of application: Compress, massage

Condition or requirement: Earache
Oil: Camomile, lavender
Method of application: Compress (warm)

Condition or requirement: Eczema
Oil: Bergamot, camomile, birch, *lavender, geranium,* hyssop, *juniper,* melissa, carrot
Method of application: Massage, bath

Condition or requirement: Exhaustion
Oil: Rosemary, bergamot
Method of application: Bath, massage

Condition or requirement: Fainting
Oil: Basil, rosemary, peppermint, lavender, neroli
Method of application: Inhalation

Condition or requirement: Fatigue
Oil: Rosemary, geranium, basil, *bergamot,* peppermint
Method of application: Bath, massage, inhalation

Condition or requirement: Fever
Oil: Basil, camomile, cypress, bergamot, melissa, eucalyptus, lavender, rosemary
Method of application: Bath

Condition or requirement: Flatulence
Oil: Black pepper, camomile, ginger, fennel, juniper, peppermint, rosemary, coriander
Method of application: Massage, compress

Condition or requirement: Flu (see Influenza)

Condition or requirement: Frigidity
Oil: Clary-sage, rose, ginger, *ylang-ylang,* cinnamon
Method of application: Bath, massage

Condition or requirement: Gallstones
Oil: Rosemary, lavender
Method of application: Massage

Condition or requirement: Gingivitis (inflamed gums)
Oil: Fennel, myrrh, thyme
Method of application: Mouthwash

Condition or requirement: Gonorrhoea
Oil: Bergamot, cedarwood, eucalyptus, lavender,
  sandalwood
Method of application: Massage, bath

Condition or requirement: Gout
Oil: Basil, benzoin, camphor, juniper, rosemary
Method of application: Massage, compress

Condition or requirement: Grief
Oil: Rose, melissa, lavender, rosewood
Method of application: Massage, bath

Condition or requirement: Haemorrhoids
Oil: Cypress, frankincense, juniper, myrrh, lavender,
  rosemary
Method of application: Bath, massage

Condition or requirement: Halitosis
Oil: Spearmint, bergamot, nutmeg, *cardamom, peppermint,*
  myrrh
Method of application: Mouthwash

Condition or requirement: Hangover
Oil: Juniper, rosemary
Method of application: Bath, massage

Condition or requirement: Hay fever
Oil: Eucalyptus, rose, lavender, melissa, camomile
Method of application: Inhalation

Condition or requirement: Headaches
Oil: Peppermint, marjoram, rose, *lavender*, rosemary,
	eucalyptus
Method of application: Compress, massage

Condition or requirement: Heart
Oil: Ylang-ylang, neroli, lavender, melissa
Method of application: Massage, bath

Condition or requirement: Heartburn
Oil: Cardamom, black pepper
Method of application: Massage

Condition or requirement: Herpes
Oil: Bergamot, eucalyptus, patchouli, *tea-tree*, lavender
Method of application: Compress

Condition or requirement: Hypertension (high blood
	pressure)
Oil: Lavender, ylang-ylang, marjoram, camomile, neroli,
	bergamot, rose
Method of application: Bath, massage

Condition or requirement: Hypotension (low blood pressure)
Oil: Rosemary, camphor, peppermint, black pepper
Method of application: Bath, massage

Condition or requirement: Hysteria
Oil: Basil, camomile, lavender, neroli, marjoram, ylang-ylang
Method of application: Inhalation, bath, massage

Condition or requirement: Impotence
Oil: Clary-sage, jasmine, ginger, rose, ylang-ylang,
	sandalwood
Method of application: Bath, massage

Condition or requirement: Indigestion
Oil: Camomile, fennel, lavender, peppermint, basil,
  marjoram, coriander
Method of application: Massage, compress

Condition or requirement: Influenza
Oil: Black pepper, niaouli, eucalyptus, rosemary,
  peppermint, garlic, tea-tree, cypress
Method of application: Inhalation

Condition or requirement: Insect bites
Oil: Lavender, eucalyptus, geranium
Method of application: Compress

Condition or requirement: Insomnia
Oil: Marjoram, lavender, camomile, neroli, sandalwood
Method of application: Bath, massage

Condition or requirement: Irritability
Oil: Lavender, camomile, neroli
Method of application: Bath, massage

Condition or requirement: Itchiness
Oil: Camomile, lavender, melissa, bergamot
Method of application: Massage, compress

Condition or requirement: Jaundice
Oil: Rosemary, camomile, thyme, peppermint
Method of application: Bath, massage

Condition or requirement: Kidneys
Oil: Juniper, sandalwood, fennel, camomile, cedarwood
Method of application: Massage, bath, compress

Condition or requirement: Laryngitis
Oil: Benzoin, sandalwood, lavender, frankincense, thyme,
  myrrh
Method of application: Inhalation

Condition or requirement: Liver
Oil: Cypress, *juniper, rose,* camomile, peppermint, cumin,
    rosemary
Method of application: Bath, compress, massage

Condition or requirement: Mastitis
Oil: Geranium, lavender, rose
Method of application: Compress, massage

Condition or requirement: Measles
Oil: Eucalyptus, tea-tree
Method of application: Inhalation, bath

Condition or requirement: Memory (poor)
Oil: Basil, rosemary, peppermint
Method of application: Inhalation

Condition or requirement: Menopause
Oil: Camomile, lavender, rose, geranium, jasmine,
    bergamot, ylang-ylang
Method of application: Bath, massage

Condition or requirement: Menstruation
Oil: Rose, melissa, myrrh, clary-sage, rosemary, marjoram,
    camomile, cypress, pine
Method of application: Compress, bath, massage

Condition or requirement: Mental fatigue
Oil: Basil, rosemary, peppermint
Method of application: Bath, inhalation

Condition or requirement: Migraine
Oil: Marjoram, peppermint, rosemary, camomile, lavender,
    basil
Method of application: Cold compress, massage

Condition or requirement: Mouth ulcers
Oil: Myrrh, orange
Method of application: Mouthwash

Condition or requirement: Muscle strain
Oil: Lavender, *ginger, rosemary*, juniper
Method of application: Massage

Condition or requirement: Nausea
Oil: Basil, *peppermint,* lavender, fennel, rose, *camomile,*
    nutmeg, spearmint
Method of application: Warm compress, massage

Condition or requirement: Nervous tension
Oil: Benzoin, camomile, lavender, neroli, patchouli, ylang-
    ylang, sandalwood
Method of application: Massage, bath

Condition or requirement: Nettle rash
Oil: Camomile, melissa
Method of application: Bath

Condition or requirement: Neuralgia
Oil: Camomile, eucalyptus, geranium, marjoram, rosemary,
    clary-sage
Method of application: Massage

Condition or requirement: Nose bleed
Oil: Cypress, *frankincense, lemon*
Method of application: Cold compress

Condition or requirement: Obesity
Oil: Fennel, juniper, rosemary, bergamot, geranium
Method of application: Massage, bath

Condition or requirement: Oedema (swelling)
Oil: Juniper, patchouli, fennel, geranium, rosemary
Method of application: Massage

Condition or requirement: Oily skin
Oil: Bergamot, lemon, mandarin, sandalwood, geranium
Method of application: Skin preparation

Condition or requirement: Palpitations
Oil: Lavender, ylang-ylang, melissa, neroli, rosemary
Method of application: Massage

Condition or requirement: Piles (see Haemorrhoids)

Condition or requirement: PMT
Oil: Geranium, ylang-ylang, bergamot, rose, camomile
Method of application: Bath, massage

Condition or requirement: Pneumonia
Oil: Cajeput, niaouli, tea-tree, eucalyptus
Method of application: Bath, inhalation

Condition or requirement: Pregnancy
Oil: Mandarin, neroli
Method of application: Bath, massage

Condition or requirement: Psoriasis
Oil: Bergamot, lavender, juniper, camomile, carrot
Method of application: Bath, compress

Condition or requirement: Pyelitis (inflammation of renal
   pelvis)
Oil: Juniper, camomile, cedarwood
Method of application: Massage

Condition or requirement: Relaxation
Oil: Lavender, neroli, ylang-ylang, rosewood, marjoram,
   rose, sandalwood, camomile, bergamot
Method of application: Massage, bath

Condition or requirement: Rheumatism
Oil: Rosemary, juniper, cypress, lavender, camomile, bay,
   marjoram, coriander
Method of application: Massage, bath

Condition or requirement: Ringworm
Oil: Geranium, myrrh, lavender, rosemary, peppermint
Method of application: Hair and skin preparations

Condition or requirement: Scabies
Oil: Lavender, camomile, lemon, bergamot, rosemary
Method of application: Bath, skin preparation

Condition or requirement: Scalds
Oil: Lavender, camomile, eucalyptus
Method of application: Compress

Condition or requirement: Sciatica
Oil: Camomile, lavender
Method of application: Massage, bath, compress

Condition or requirement: Sensitive skin
Oil: Camomile, neroli, *rose,* sandalwood
Method of application: Skin preparation

Condition or requirement: Shingles
Oil: Eucalyptus, geranium, bergamot, tea-tree, peppermint
Method of application: Bath

Condition or requirement: Shock
Oil: Camphor, neroli, peppermint
Method of application: Inhalation

Condition or requirement: Sickness (see Vomiting)

Condition or requirement: Sinusitis
Oil: Eucalyptus, peppermint, niaouli, rosemary, bay,
   lavender, pine
Method of application: Inhalation

Condition or requirement: Skin (see Dry skin, Oily skin and
   Sensitive skin)

Condition or requirement: Snakebite
Oil: Lavender, basil, tea-tree
Method of application: Compress

Condition or requirement: Sore throat
Oil: Benzoin, sandalwood, lavender, eucalyptus, niaouli, pine
Method of application: Inhalation, gargle

Condition or requirement: Sprains
Oil: Eucalyptus, lavender, rosemary, camomile, marjoram
Method of application: Cold compress

Condition or requirement: Stomach
Oil: Fennel, peppermint, lavender, mandarin, orange, camomile
Method of application: Compress, massage

Condition or requirement: Stress
Oil: Lavender, sandalwood, ylang-ylang, rose
Method of application: Bath, massage

Condition or requirement: Stretch marks
Oil: Mandarin, tangerine
Method of application: Massage

Condition or requirement: Sunburn
Oil: Lavender, camomile
Method of application: Compress, bath

Condition or requirement: Teething (babies)
Oil: Camomile
Method of application: Massage

Condition or requirement: Thread veins
Oil: Cypress
Method of application: Massage

Condition or requirement: Throat (laryngitis)
Oil: Sandalwood, benzoin
Method of application: Inhalation

Condition or requirement: Thrush
Oil: Myrrh, sandalwood, lavender, tea-tree
Method of application: Douche, sitz bath

Condition or requirement: Tonsillitis
Oil: Lavender, benzoin
Method of application: Inhalation

Condition or requirement: Toothache
Oil: Clove, camomile
Method of application: Compress, cotton bud

Condition or requirement: Travel sickness
Oil: Peppermint
Method of application: Inhalation

Condition or requirement: Ulcers (body; see also Mouth ulcers)
Oil: Garlic
Method of application: Compress

Condition or requirement: Urethritis
Oil: Bergamot, lavender
Method of application: Bath, massage

Condition or requirement: Varicose veins
Oil: Cypress, geranium
Method of application: Compress, gentle massage

Condition or requirement: Verrucae (see Warts)

Condition or requirement: Vertigo
Oil: Basil, rosemary, peppermint, black pepper
Method of application: Inhalation

Condition or requirement: Vomiting
Oil: Fennel, peppermint, rose, camomile
Method of application: Compress, gentle massage

Condition or requirement: Warts (verrucae)
Oil: Tea-tree, lemon, thuja
Method of application: Cotton bud, compress

Condition or requirement: Water retention
Oil: Geranium, *juniper*, parsley, *clary-sage, fennel*, pine,
   sage, violet leaves
Method of application: Bath, massage

Condition or requirement: Whooping cough
Oil: Basil, cypress, rosemary, niaouli, lavender, tea-tree
Method of application: Inhalation, massage

Condition or requirement: Worms
Oil: Bergamot, camomile, eucalyptus, lavender
Method of application: Massage, compress

Condition or requirement: Wounds
Oil: Benzoin, lavender, olibanum, eucalyptus, tea-tree
Method of application: Compress

Condition or requirement: Wrinkles
Oil: Frankincense, lemon, sandalwood
Method of application: Skin preparation

USEFUL ADDRESSES

If you cannot find a local shop selling the oils or if you are dubious about the quality, the following companies all supply excellent oils by mail order. Write for a price list, enclosing a stamped addressed envelope.

The Essential Touch
c/o 108b Haverstock Hill
London NW3
(For oils)

Anita Philips Aromatherapy Ltd
Sarnett House
Gidea Park
Essex
RM2 5LP
(Tel. 0708–720 289)
(For oils, and hair and skin products)

Essentially Yours
PO Box 38
Romford
Essex
RM1 DN
(For oils, formulas and diffusers)

Aromatherapy course information

Nicole Perez
The School of Holistic Aromatherapy
108b Haverstock Hill
London NW3

V. Worwood
PO Box 38
Romford
Essex
RM1 DN

American Aromatherapy Association
PO Box 3609
Culver City
California 90231
USA

Berida Manor
PO Box 350
Bowral
New South Wales 2576
Australia

International Federation of Aromatherapists
4 Eastmearn Road
London SE21 8HA

Massage course information

The Churchill Centre
22 Montagu Street
London W1
(Tel. 071–402 9475)

If you want to do massage regularly a couch is a good investment. You can order one from the above address custom-built to suit your height.

Details of local practitioners

The International Federation of Aromatherapists (address above) regularly publishes newsletters containing information on events, books, and research related to aromatherapy. It also often holds lectures on the subject. If you wish to become a member and be put on their mailing list, write to them for information or simply apply for a list of practitioners in your area.

FURTHER READING

Worwood, Valerie Ann, *The Fragrant Pharmacy*
(Macmillan).
Valnet, Dr Jean, *The Practice of Aromatherapy* (C. W. Daniel
Co. Ltd)
Ryman, Daniele, *The Aromatherapy Handbook* (C. W. Daniel
Co. Ltd)
Tisserand, Robert, *The Art of Aromatherapy* (C. W. Daniel
Co. Ltd)